T0265643

URCHIN
ON THE
BEAT

The Tale of a Bad Adolescence
& Its Joyful Conclusion

URCHIN
ON THE BEAT

Uwe Siemon-Netto

Urchin on the Beat: The Tale of a Bad Adolescence and its Joyful Conclusion

© 2024 New Reformation Publications

Published by:
1517 Publishing
PO Box 54032
Irvine, CA 92619-4032

Publisher's Cataloging-In-Publication Data

Names: Siemon-Netto, Uwe, author.
Title: Urchin on the beat : the tale of a bad adolescence and its joyful conclusion / by Uwe Siemon-Netto.
Description: Irvine, CA : 1517 Publishing, [2024] | Series: [The urchin series] ; [2] | Includes bibliographical references.
Identifiers: ISBN: 978-1-962654-64-7 (hardcover) | 978-1-962654-65-4 (paperback) | 978-1-962654-66-1 (ebook) | 978-1-962654-67-8 (audiobook)
Subjects: LCSH: Siemon-Netto, Uwe—Childhood and youth. | World War, 1939-1945—Personal narratives, German. | Journalists—Germany—Biography. | Teenagers—Germany—History—20th century. | Lutheran Church—Germany—History—20th century. | LCGFT: Autobiographies. | BISAC: BIOGRAPHY & AUTOBIOGRAPHY / Editors, Journalists, Publishers. | BIOGRAPHY & AUTOBIOGRAPHY / Memoirs. | RELIGION / Christianity / Lutheran.
Classification: LCC: D811.5.S534 A3 2024 | DDC: 940.54/8243--dc23

Printed in the United States of America.

Cover art by Zachariah James Stuef.

Contents

Farewell to Gillian

SADLY, I MUST PRECEDE the chronological order of my autobiography with an homage to my late wife, Gillian, who died on the fourth of March 2022 after a glorious marriage of nearly 60 years. A lovely episode from New York describes best how close we were. We sat in a bus from East 55th Street to Chinatown when an inebriated black man moved up to us with a broad smile and asked,

"How long have youse guys been married?"

"Thirty-eight years," we answered in unison.

"Thirty-eight years! Wow! I thought so! You look like identical twins, like two peas in a pod. It's funny how happily married couples eventually look alike. My parents were like that, which was a beautiful thing—beautiful and very rare. It would be an honor to sit next to you. May I?"

"Please sit with us. It would be fun to have you as our travel companion on this long trip."

"Where are you going?" he asked.

"To celebrate Chinese New Year with friends from Hong Kong."

"Wow! You have friends from Hong Kong?"

"Many. We used to live there."

"Wow! Real Chinese friends?"

"Of course!"

"Wow!"

He got off after a few stops, but we never forgot this lovely encounter with a total stranger because his remarks defined our union. The harmony between us became manifest in a magnet Gillian stuck to the door of our refrigerator only a few years ago. It reads, "Happiness is being married to a German." I wonder how many of my fellow countrymen have been honored with this award, to which my response can sadly be a mere oxymoron, an unwritten postscript: "Happiness was being married to *this* Englishwoman."

I am often asked, "What kept the two of you together for such a long time?" I answer, "Not once in our marriage did we go to bed in anger; we always made up before falling asleep." This inevitably prompts a follow-up question: "How did you do that?"

"Humor," I say, "a mutual sense of hilarity, taking the mickey out of ourselves." Though hailing from different cultures, we had the gift of cracking one-liners, which made both of us laugh and thus deflated the fight. Nothing, not even the most overwhelming reasons for anger—of which we had plenty—could trump the realization that, in the end, we humans are all blithering fools. This is an ontological state that can only be surmounted with laughter.

How did this miraculous union originate? It had, in a sense, a mirthful genesis. I was stationed in London as a young foreign correspondent for Axel Springer Verlag, the biggest West German publishing house. I was 25 then and had found delight in the arms of an exotic creature. She was Lebanese, had long black hair, deep and wet black eyes, luscious lips, and a smokey voice that was a perfect fit for her superb French. She was also a brilliant pianist; nothing was more exhilarating than to hear and watch her play Chopin on a Blüthner grand in her Eve's clothing, her ample behind wobbling merrily on top of my only valuable possession at the time: a first edition of Baudelaire. She was called Emily, a name rooted in the Greek vocable, *aimylos*, meaning "wily" or "persuasive"—two adjectives that fit her well.

There was nothing wrong with Emily other than that her lifestyle and values seemed incompatible with those of a young international reporter at the beginning of a promising career. In my few thinking moments in between being besotted by my wondrous lover, I realized: It can either be Emily or work. If I opted for the former, I would do so at the risk of dropping out of my profession; then again, if I pursued my glamorous calling, I would surely lose Emily. This raised the question: How was I to disentangle myself from this perilous affair, in which my libidinous nature thoroughly regaled?

The solution came in the person of Gillian. On a Saturday morning in early May 1962, our telephone rang. A silvery voice I had never heard before, said, "I am hungry!"

"Come over. I am just about to make spaghetti," I said. It was 11:30 a.m., and Emily was still asleep after twisting and rocking all night in assorted nightclubs.

The doorbell rang, and in walked Gillian Ackers, clad in a Mexican poncho, her peach-colored, round face smiling. She was the quintessential Englishwoman: bubbly, chipper, wholesome, full of good humor. I was in love. Ever the reporter, I questioned her with as much charm as a German reporter could muster.

I found out that she hailed from Southampton, gateway to the British Empire, where she was bombed out by the naughty Luftwaffe ("Ah, what a coincidence: I was bombed out by the Royal Air Force," I interjected). Her mother was a piano teacher with a preference for Bach, and her father was the former head wine steward on the *Queen Mary* but now the publican of the Ham & Blackbird, including the Railway Hotel, in Farnborough, Hampshire.

She had studied art at Guildford College, was a stage designer for an ad agency, then worked for *Vogue* magazine before becoming the manageress of Stockpots, a chain of greasy spoons owned by her then-boyfriend. But just now, she had returned from a one-year stay in Mexico and the United States, was out of money, and was very hungry—before eating my noodles and tomato sauce!

I was in love, and Emily was still asleep.

That Saturday afternoon, I was on duty, having to handle the news flow from our New York bureau and other parts of the English-speaking world and, of course, being expected to contribute stories of my own from Britain for our Sunday papers in Hamburg, West Berlin, and Düsseldorf. My office was in the *Daily Telegraph* building on Fleet Street. I offered to drop Gillian off at her Chelsea flat.

We sneaked out, and Emily was still asleep.

"What is it like working at that building? Stuffy, isn't it?" Gillian asked me as I helped her into my absurd-looking car, a grey Citroën 2CV with a 375-cc engine and a body of corrugated sheet metal resembling a Paris public lavatory on wheels.

"Unpleasant," I answered, "they really do hate Germans there."

"How do they show it?"

"Not a day goes by without people peeing against our office door next to the lavatory."

"This is so disgusting, so un-English! My friends and I want the exact opposite. We have, like you, suffered horribly during the war. All we want now is to love each other and to be part of one united Europe as Churchill had urged us all." She was referring to his famous Zürich speech in 1946.

"I agree."

Years later, we both remembered this dialogue with tears in our eyes when driven by hate-mongering London newspapers (including the *Daily Telegraph*), the British voted in 2016 to secede from the European Union. We realized that our love had outlasted one of the most brilliant alliances in history. Jingoism had trumped it.

When I dropped Gillian off at her Burton Court flat, I asked her, "Would you like to dine with me tonight?"

"Yes, I would enjoy that, but at what time? If I'm not called by nine in the evening, I go to bed. Period."

"Gillian, as a journalist, I am not master of my time; the news flow is. I'll call as soon as I am free."

"Please do that. I am looking forward to it," she answered with a sunny smile before rushing into the house.

It so happened that I received my last copy from New York shortly before 11:00 p.m. I quickly edited it and had it telexed to Hamburg at eleven. Then I called Gillian.

"I'll be showered and dressed and waiting for you," she said matter-of-factly.

We went for a sturdy meal in an all-night Jewish nosh bar off Piccadilly, which was open now as the Sabbath was over. Then we twisted until four in the morning at the Saddle Room in Park Lane, London's first discothèque. It was a fancy place owned by Hélène Cordet, Prince Philip's childhood friend from Greece. When we entered, I made out Princess Margaret, the Queen's sister, in the arms of a companion. The photograph in this chapter, showing Gillian and me in a loving embrace, was taken in the Saddle Room that night.

We drove to Gillian's flat almost at dawn. I moved in and never moved out again, figuratively speaking.

A few weeks later, she introduced me to her parents. Her father, Sidney Ackers, greeted me with the words, "The only good German is a dead German." When he saw the shock in my face, he jumped up, laughed, and said, "That was just a stupid joke, you silly bugger, let me hug you. You are welcome in my family!"

He held me for a long, long time, saying, "From now on, you are part of us, you understand? You are safe with us, as we know that Gillian will be safe with you. You will find that, from now on, you will be our son. We love you as our child, don't we, Ethel?"

"Yes," said Ethel Ackers, whose maiden name, Kneen, indicated that her family roots were in the Isle of Man, a self-governing British Crown Dependency in the Irish Sea. Like all the Manx, Ethel was a Celt, quite different from her southern English husband.

She, too, was humorous but in a sharp-witted, sometimes biting way, swift to strike verbally, wonderful to fence with, but at heart rock solid, just like Sidney. The greatest of the many gifts Sidney and Ethel gave Gillian was to teach her, by their example, how to conduct a proper marriage for the benefit of their only child. And Gillian passed this on to me; she taught me to love.

Before living with Gillian, I had thought I would never enjoy an enduring marriage by the side of a steadfast woman. I didn't even know what that meant! I didn't experience it in my childhood, which was essentially a single-parent infancy, the single parent being Omi, my magnificent maternal grandmother. But Mutti, my mother, and

Vati, my war-blinded father? They were too self-absorbed to show their only child the joys of a healthy family life.

Oh, don't get me wrong. They saw to it that I could conduct myself in polite society. When I was six, I learned how to unobtrusively turn the pianist's pages at my family's home concerts. I had been taught to kiss a lady's hand like a gentleman, not slobber all over it but just carefully raise it to my slightly bowed head, lower my lips to just one or two millimeters above her skin, noiselessly emulate a kiss, and smile. I had learned how to greet a gentleman by standing straight, clicking my heels, and looking him straight in the eyes as I shook his right hand firmly.

By the time I entered elementary school, I knew that a well-brought-up male would never sit down before the last lady in the room had taken her place. I knew how to help my dinner partner, adult or otherwise, into her chair, and how not to place my arms beyond the wrists on the dinner table. I knew how to understand the arrangement of the silverware before me, how to hold a knife and fork properly, and how to alternate my attention between the ladies on my right and my left.

All this and much more I was taught, and for it, I am—to this day—filled with gratitude. However, I was deprived of the essential subject to which I should have been introduced, especially in the horrific war that marked my childhood: family love.

It took Gillian to teach me that. Mourning her, I cannot hold back the tears while remembering her ultimate graduation gift at the completion of this 60-year course. Whenever, in her last years, I passed her seat or her side of the bed, she grabbed my hand and said, "Thank you, Uwe, thank you, thank you, thank you!"

Much more about Gillian will be said in the next volume of this *Urchin* series. But right now, I must discuss briefly one hugely important point about her: Gillian's faith. She was outwardly a gregarious woman, but it took me six decades to plumb the inner Gillian. She was an Englishwoman, and Englishwomen of her kind are not in the habit of letting their souls hang out for all to see.

Was she a Christian woman? I only discovered to what extent she was that while attending the Lutheran School of Theology at Chicago late in our lives. She audited some of my classes, especially Systematic Theology and the Lutheran Confessions, where we learned to distinguish Law and Gospel within the larger context of Luther's doctrine of the Two Kingdoms.

"Finally, the penny has dropped," she said joyfully as we headed home for dinner. "Luther has taught me what our Church of England vicar never manages to explain to me convincingly. Now I know the central point of my Christian faith: We are forgiven sinners."

In her last months, she never failed to speak the Lord's Prayer with me, if only by moving her lips. Four days before she died, our irreplaceable Pastor Ron Hodel, who himself passed away a few weeks after Gillian at the age of only 66 years, brought her the Lord's Supper. She moved her lips to the Prayer of Confession and audibly answered "yes" when Pastor Ron asked her whether she was sorry for her sins and wanted God's grace and mercy, and again when he said, "Do you believe that the forgiveness I speak is not my forgiveness, but God's?"

And finally, when he proclaimed, "Go in peace," she said clearly, "Amen!"

This was the last word my Gillian ever spoke.

R.I.P.

Introduction

Urchin's Rollercoaster

Ich bin ein rechtes Rabenaas,

ein wahrer Sündenknüppel,

der seine Sünden in sich fraß,

als wie der Russ die Zwibbel.

O Herr, so nimm mich

Hund bei'm Ohr,

wirf mir den Gnadenknochen vor

und stoß mich Sündenlümmel

in deinen Gnadenhimmel!

I am a right carrion for the ravens,

A real cripple of sin,

Who ate his sins within himself,

As a Russian does his onions.

O Lord, so take me,

Dog by the ear,

Throw me a bone of mercy,

And push me, sinful scoundrel,

to your heaven of grace!

I FOUND THIS AMUSING anthem in an old Silesian hymnal. It will be the *leitmotiv* of this second volume of my *Urchin* series, for it fits the rollercoaster of my life following my brief childhood as an urchin at war.

My childhood ended with my escape from Soviet-occupied Leipzig at the age of 10 and my separation from Omi, my maternal grandmother. Omi had taught me, during World War II, to be always fearless, even when bombs were detonating all around us. To show fear, she said, was un-Christian and ungentlemanly.

In my thorny adolescence, I discovered how sound this advice was, although I often had reasons to despair. Under Omi's supervision in Leipzig, I was among the best in my class at elementary school. Separated from her in West Germany, I dropped out of high school with disgraceful grades in mathematics and Latin. Great was the temptation to just give up.

Yet by the time I reached 19, I was a promising trainee reporter and, two years later, a multilingual "slot editor" at the Frankfurt bureau of the Associated Press. After another three years, I became a foreign correspondent covering world events, including the construction of the Berlin Wall, the Cuban missile crisis, the assassination of President John F. Kennedy, and the war in Vietnam. That went fast, although it took me much longer to complete my education, as I had promised myself when I was still a teenager. I was 55 years old when I earned my Ph.D. at Boston University.

All this I attribute at least partly to Omi's wartime pedagogy, which steeled me against all temptations to surrender and trained me to be a lifelong urchin: impish, yes; cowardly, no.

Omi's guidance proved particularly powerful in matters of faith. Not that I became a fervent churchgoer after we were separated on

10 August 1947. In fact, for a long time, I relegated the loving God of Christianity to the waiting room of my biography. Still, I never stopped believing in Him because He made infinitely more sense than the esoteric gobbledygook permeating the three Rudolf Steiner schools my parents carelessly sent me to for the next eight years.

Remembering Omi's theology courses in her air raid shelter shielded me against worrying about Kamaloca, the state where, according to Steiner, my astral body would be parked after the death of my fleshly self until my reincarnation.

To me, Kamaloca seemed a dismal place where the dead supposedly suffer for all their misdeeds and for precisely the length of time they had committed them. I preferred not to think about the consequences for my astral body of the terror my impish pranks had inflicted on Leipzig tram conductors. Better not to concern myself with my astral body, if indeed I had one, and to stick with the forgiving God of Christianity and never mind Steiner.

God eventually emerged from my waiting room and took me "dog by the ear," as the Silesian hymn put it so drolly. However, this story will not be told until a subsequent tome of my *Urchin* series. In the present volume, I shall unfold the helter-skelter of my high school years and my early career as a journalist, periods in which I nevertheless derived some comfort from remaining a rascal, albeit never an entirely godless one.

CHAPTER 1

Yarn on Wheels

THE NEW PHASE IN my young life dawned on Christmas Day, 1947, the last my parents and I spent together as a family. It was a bizarre reunion that made me realize my childhood was definitely over. I was eleven years old.

I concluded Volume I of my autobiographical *Urchin* series with this saddest Noël of my young life thus far. To summarize: My divorced parents and I met in a modest inn in Neu-Ulm, the little Bavarian sister city of Ulm, which is part of the German state of Baden-Württemberg. We arrived from three different directions: Mutti, my mother, had sneaked across the border from Leipzig in the Soviet zone. Vati, my father, had taken a leave of absence from an Allied establishment in Kirchheim-an-der-Jagst (near Stuttgart), where the Americans groomed candidates for senior positions in the new West German administration they and the British were creating. I came from a Lutheran deaconess hospital in Schwäbisch-Hall, where I had been dumped for a whooping cough I did not have.

We spent Christmas Eve by a small pine tree in Vati's room. I received some gifts before Mutti dispatched me to the neighboring room she and I shared.

"Vati and I have something to discuss. Go to bed now, Uwe. I will join you soon," she said.

Of course, I did not go to bed but remained in the corridor, pressing my ear against Vati's door.

I heard him tell my mother that the British had offered him a top job in the regional government of Eastern Westphalia and Lippe in Detmold, a beautiful city close to Lage, where he was born. Vati said he would only accept if Mutti agreed to reconstitute their marriage for my sake. My mother refused, whereupon my father informed her that in that case, he would take early retirement.

The next morning, Mutti returned to Leipzig, leaving it to my father to take me to Schloß Hamborn, a boarding school in a 19th-century castle near the cathedral city of Paderborn, not far from Demold and Lage, where he would visit relatives.

Lily Eckart, his former lady friend, drove Vati and me in her Hillman to the bomb-shattered *Hauptbahnhof* (central station) of Ulm. For the first time since becoming my foster mother on 11 August 1947, this stern Swiss woman showed a little tenderness. She stroked my head and said:

"You are a lucky little man, Uwe. You are leaving by luxury train while all other Germans travel on running boards, bumpers, coal tenders, and carriage roofs."

I gave her a thankful smile, not knowing that I owed her much more gratitude, for Auntie Lily secretly paid for my tuition at boarding school for the next four years. She withheld this information from me until years later.

We had a little time to pass until our departure. We took a table in the station restaurant, where I overheard a sordid conversation suggesting the blossoming of German-American fraternization forbidden by Gen. Dwight D. Eisenhower at the end of the war. At the table next to ours, a bleary-eyed young German woman's left hand rubbed an American soldier's right thigh.

"Okay, okay, darling?" the woman sighed for all in the room to hear. "*First vee heff another Cola and zen vee make a numbah.*"

My father's facial expression, hitherto grim, changed into a grin. Lily Eckart gave Vati a disapproving look, which, of course, he couldn't see. Later, on our trip north, he decoded the woman's remark for me to an extent suitable for an eleven-year-old boy. This much I understood, though: To "make a number" was an awkward English translation of the crude German idiom, "*eine Nummer machen*," referring to lustful activity.

We went to the platform. A glistening train from Munich arrived on its way north. It resembled the luxurious DUS Express for Allied personnel (and Germans with special passes) on which Mutti and I had traveled from Kassel to Ulm after our escape from the Soviet zone on 11 August 1947. The one difference between the two journeys was that Mutti and I were allowed on board by the grace of a kindly U.S. female officer. Vati, by contrast, had an official permit.

"Vati, how did you get tickets for this train?" I asked him.

"The Americans gave them to me," he answered but did not elaborate.

Freshly painted and not very full, the train's carriages were a stunning contrast to the woefully crowded, rusty, and dented choo choos on the other tracks. Those still bore pockmarks from the war, whilst our express gave us a foretaste of the peace and prosperity to come. It even had a red restaurant car, one of the handful that had survived the Third Reich.

German express trains were divided into three classes, ranging from modest cabins with wooden slat benches to luxurious mahogany-paneled coupés with four deep armchairs each. We were assigned two of six nicely upholstered seats in an otherwise empty second-class coupé.

With a piercing whine, an electric locomotive pulled our train through bombed-out suburbs, towns, and villages on its way to Stuttgart and beyond. I pressed my nose against the window, fascinated by the chilling scenes gliding past us. So many homes, churches, and factories on both sides of the tracks were damaged or destroyed. Occasionally, I spotted a Christmas tree on the tarpaulin-covered rump of what must have been a multistoried apartment building; the other floors were gone. I described these scenes to Vati until the dining room porter's gong invited passengers to proceed to their tables for lunch. Anticipating a decent wine, Vati smiled instantly as we joined other passengers on their way to the restaurant. Most spoke English. Some wore smart foreign uniforms, others well-cut suits and dresses.

The tables in the restaurant car were covered with starched linens and festively decorated for Christmas with pine branches.

"A drink, Herr Doktor?" the steward asked after checking Vati's ID. He was a distinguished-looking gentleman about my father's age. Like my father, he wore a World War I *Verwundetenabzeichen* (wound badge) on the left side of his white jacket. The steward stared at Vati's chest but didn't mention the common fate the two men had suffered in their youth. Vati ordered two bottles of Moselle.

"May I serve you one now and bring the other to your compartment later, Herr Doktor?"

"Yes, thank you," answered my father, now in a merry mood.

"At your service, Herr Doktor."

I can't recall what we had for lunch because a much more memorable scene followed. Perhaps we had beef goulash with *spätzle* and a cucumber salad followed by a vanilla pudding with chocolate sauce, standard German comfort fare.

After lunch, the steward helped me guide my father back to our compartment. Suddenly, he stopped. He stared at Vati's left cheek and said,

"This must be painful, Herr Doktor."

"What?"

"The boil on your cheek. It looks like a piece of shrapnel is about to pop out."

"How do you know that?" my father asked him, perplexed.

"I have the same problems ever since I was hit in 1917."

"Where were you wounded?"

"In the Vosges."

"So was I," Vati said.

"Allow me to relieve you of this," the steward continued. "I have the necessary instruments on this train. I'll be back momentarily."

When he returned, he transformed our compartment into a small operating theater. He disinfected the nasty-looking boil, lanced it with a surgical knife, disinfected the wound again, and quickly removed a small piece of metal with a pair of tweezers. My father did not flinch. The steward cleaned out the wound, covered it with a large band-aid, gave Vati a painkiller, and said,

"That should do it, Herr Doktor. I'll be back later with your second bottle of wine. Meanwhile, try to get some sleep."

"What a fine soldier you are!" Vati said as softly as I had ever heard him speak before.

"On occasions like this, I sense that my military experience has at least some merit, Herr Doktor," the steward replied. "I was trained in first aid."

When the steward returned, he saw that my father was reaching for his wallet in his jacket, obviously intending to give the steward a gratuity.

"*Nein, nein, Herr Doktor!*" he said firmly, "Wounded veterans don't tip each other for acts of solidarity. Rest a little more. I'll see you later."

"What an exceptional gentleman!" exclaimed Vati after the steward had left. He nodded off again.

When he woke, he suddenly became talkative, animated by his first glass from the second bottle the steward had deposited on the small table in front of his seat. I asked him, "Our tickets say we are going to Hamburg. Is Schloß Hamborn, my boarding school, near Hamburg?"

"No. I will take you there after New Year's Day, but first we will celebrate with my friends, the Klügmanns."

"The Klügmanns?"

Vati broke into the kind of inebriated smile I loved most about him because it always foreshadowed a good tale; he was a marvelous raconteur.

"This is going to be a long, 'shaggy dog' story, as the English say, Uwe, *eine Zottelhundgeschichte* about a young lady who should have become your mother and would have made both of us happy," he said.

"Why is she not my mother?"

"I made a mistake."

"Which was?"

"Breaking my engagement with this woman and marrying somebody else."

"Mutti?"

"Yes."

"Why did you do this, Vati?"

"I met your mother at the annual ball of Thuringia Leipzig, my student fraternity. All my fraternity brothers assured me that your mother was the most beautiful lady in the room. She was young and very crisp. She wore a beautiful perfume and was a delight to waltz with. I liked all that. In fact, I was besotted by her."

"How did you meet the Klügmanns?" I asked him after our train had left Stuttgart and was now speeding north, pulled by a Model 01 steam locomotive that had replaced our electric engine. The Model 01 was licensed to travel at a top speed of 139 km (~86 miles) per hour.

"Long before you were born," my father began, "I spent several weeks each summer in a clinic owned by Count Maximilian von Wise, a celebrated ophthalmologist who tried to make me see again. First, Count Wise practiced in Thuringia, where I met Lily. Then he moved to Bad Eilsen, a spa in Lower Saxony. What I am about to tell you happened perhaps in 1928 or 1929."

According to Vati, Bad Eilsen had a fine *Kurhaus* (health resort) with a renowned dining room where, at one lunch hour, the maître d'hôtel led him to a table of three ladies, a mother and her two daughters, whom this headwaiter had overheard discussing the good looks and superbly tailored summer suit of my suntanned but blind father.

"Herr Doktor, may I introduce you to Frau Klügmann?" the headwaiter said. My father bowed and kissed her right hand.

"Herr Doktor, this is Fräulein Annemarie Klügmann," said the headwaiter; she gave Vati her left hand, and he kissed it.

"... and this, Herr Doktor, is Fräulein Renate Klügmann." Vati bowed and kissed her right hand.

"You speak such an exquisite German!" he complimented them. As a North German, he had always loathed the grotesque dialect of Leipzig, where fate had dumped him as a child.

"We are from Hamburg," answered Frau Klügmann, whose first name was Marianne.

When the main course arrived, Vati turned to her daughter Annemarie, who sat on his right, and addressed her in the gentlemanly manner of the period: *"Gnädiges Fräulein* (gracious young lady), would you cut my meat for me, please? I am blind."

"Herr Doktor, I would love to cut your meat for you. But I cannot because I am lame."

"Annemarie has just recovered from polio, which paralyzed her right arm," her mother explained.

"But my sister Renate, who sits on your left, would be delighted to cut your meat," said Annemarie.

Thus began the romance between Fräulein Renate Klügmann, nicknamed Natti, and Dr. Karl-Heinz Oskar Eduard Siemon.

Vati smiled melancholically. "We were in love," he said.

"Did you get engaged?"

"We came very close. Soon after my return from Bad Eilsen to Leipzig, Marianne Klügmann, the mother, invited me to meet her husband in their family home in Hamburg. Dr. Karl Klügmann was a lawyer and the senator (cabinet minister) representing the three Hanseatic city-states of Hamburg, Bremen, and Lübeck at the seat of the Reich government in Berlin. I went. We clicked, and Dr. Klügmann consented to Natti's and my engagement."

"And then?"

"The following winter, I met your mother at that fatal fraternity ball. Soon, we were engaged despite your Omi's objection. Your mother was still underage then. But her father granted her permission to marry me."

"Why did he do that?"

"I let him teach me to play the violin. This won him over. He was already a little senile. I never mastered the fiddle, though."

"Why did you choose Mutti over Natti?"

"Because your mother was younger than Natti," said Vati, point blank and with a sad smile.

"But now we are traveling to Natti's family. So, she must have forgiven you. Has she?" I asked Vati, whose notorious preference for crisp young girls was his defining attribute, as I later found out.

(A psychologist who knew him well surmised that this was so because the only woman he'd made love to with seeing eyes was a lissome young lady he'd met in Constance, just days before being blinded in combat in France. "Because of this, your father never learned to appreciate the sex appeal of a mature woman; this was his tragedy," the psychologist told me).

"No, Natti never forgave me," said my father with a sigh, "but her family did. Natti met a traveling salesman from Heidelberg. His name is Mundus. Natti's mother thought him such a revolting little philistine that she wouldn't even allow him to kiss his bride during their engagement luncheon. '*Mundus, lass das!*' (Mundus, don't do that), she told him in disgust. Mother Klügmann loved me, though, and invited me frequently to her husband's family home at Harvestehuder Weg 24 at the Alster River in Hamburg, where we are going now. The

Klügmanns have just returned to Hamburg for the first time since the war."

"Where were they, Vati?"

"The women had moved to the Klügmanns' summer home in Lindau, a Belle Epoque villa on the shores of Lake Constance. Dr. Klügmann and his son-in-law, Paul Schmidt, were working in Paris; Paul is the husband of Annemarie Klügmann. Remember? Annemarie was the young lady who could not cut my meat because of her paralyzed right arm. There is an amazing story behind all this."

"Tell me, Vati," I begged him. He was a wonderful storyteller, especially when tipsy.

"Dr. Klügmann was appointed public trustee of enemy assets in occupied Paris; Paul Schmidt was his right-hand man."

"What did 'trustees of enemy assets' do?"

"Klügmann and Schmidt managed the French branches of businesses owned by citizens or corporations of countries with which we were at war, for example, Burberry's, the British luxury clothiers. They had a factory in Paris. Do you remember the trench coat I loved so much before we were bombed out on 4 December 1943? That was a Burberry. It burned with the rest of most of my clothes."

"Yes, I remember the coat. Were Dr. Klügmann and Paul Schmidt Nazis, then?"

"Definitely not!" my father replied. "They were honorable businessmen in the ancient Hanseatic[1] tradition, the very opposite of

---

1 My father was referring to the traditions of the commercial and defensive confederation of merchant guilds and market towns in Northwestern and Central Europe. Growing from a few North German towns, especially Lübeck, in the late 1100s, the Hanseatic League dominated Baltic maritime trade for three centuries. Its spirit is still alive in Hanseatic cities, two of which, Hamburg and Bremen, remain autonomous states of Germany.

Nazi brutes. They were made trustees under an international treaty protecting civilian property in times of war. Their allegiance was to the rightful owners of these facilities, with whom they communicated through the International Red Cross."

"Who paid them?"

"They took their salaries and expenses out of the profits they had generated. These profits were huge because some well-managed businesses boomed in occupied Paris, and Dr. Klügmann was an outstanding executive.

"What happened to Dr. Klügmann and Paul Schmidt when the Wehrmacht was driven out of Paris?"

"They stayed behind to hand business records to the owners of the companies they had managed. The proprietors were so impressed by how much money these German trustees had made for them during the occupation that they and the French authorities asked Dr. Klügmann and Paul Schmidt: 'Why don't you just stay here and continue your good work?'"

"Why didn't they, Vati?"

"As Dr. Klügmann told the French, 'We have families in Germany. They will go straight to concentration camps if we remain in Paris. So, please open the front for us. We must be with our loved ones, whatever Germany's fate."

"Did the Allies open the front for them?"

"Yes, amazingly, they did that with permission signed by the French military commandant of Paris, a general of Alsatian origin named Marie-Pierre Koenig," my father said.

The two men's trip to their families' summer home in southern Germany was an extraordinary adventure. I can only give an imprecise description cobbled together from what my father and members of the Klügmann family told me. Evidently, they traveled with white flags on the fenders of their car under the auspices of the International Red Cross (IRC) through neutral Switzerland.

On the first day of their journey, they ran into such violent fighting at a section of the front just east of Paris that they had to return to the French capital for one night. On the next day, they tried a more southerly route where a motley troop of Communist resistance fighters stopped them and briefly took them prisoner, despite their travel permits issued by the French high command in Paris.

Further on, Wehrmacht patrols, distrustful of two German civilians in a black Citroën with IRC white flags, blocked them but, after a long palaver, allowed them to move on, presumably to the Swiss border. I am not so sure whether the Swiss were happy to let two German civilians transit their country, but then they had to because Geneva was the seat of the International Red Cross.

Eventually, Klügmann and Schmidt arrived in peaceful Lindau and stayed put while Hamburg, their hometown, was still being bombed. According to U.S. President Harry S. Truman, some 135,000 civilians died in the multiple Allied air raids on this city, more than twice as many as England lost in the German air war against their entire country. There was no point for the Klügmann family in returning to Hamburg until long after the fighting had ceased.

Germany surrendered on 7 May 1945 and was divided into an American, a British, and a Soviet zone of occupation. Two months later, the U.S. ceded a part of its zone to the French. This strip included Lindau County, which borders Austria and is situated opposite the

Swiss side of Lake Constance. Gen. Marie-Pierre Koenig became French military governor in Germany.

My father and the Klügmann family were a little hazy in their timing of what happened next. But one morning, two uniformed Frenchmen, a captain and a sergeant, rang the doorbell at the house in Lindau. The Klügmanns' maid opened.

"May we speak to Dr. Klügmann and Herr Schmidt?" the captain asked, smiling.

"Please come in," said the maid.

Before entering the foyer, the captain handed his service revolver to the sergeant because it would have been ungentlemanly to visit a civilian home bearing arms. When Klügmann came down from the dining room where he had been eating his breakfast, the captain snapped to attention.

"Are we under arrest?" asked Klügmann.

"Not at all!" the Frenchman assured him. "We just would like to take you and your son-in-law on a little trip so you can meet someone you already know. Would you please pack an overnight case? We'll bring you back here in a couple of days."

"Shall I ask our maid to make sandwiches for our journey?" Klügmann asked.

"No, we have plenty of food for all of us in the car."

Klügmann and Schmidt entered the French staff car. The sergeant drove hell-for-leather[2] northwest on near-empty roads. In the late afternoon, they arrived in Baden-Baden, the seat of the French military government, where the captain took Klügmann and Schmidt straight to the office of Gen. Koenig, the governor.

---

2 Meaning "as fast as possible."

"Ah, Dr. Klügmann!" Koenig said, "thank you for your good work as a trustee in Nazi-occupied Paris. Now we have a new assignment for you: Please act as trustee of Nazi-owned properties in the French-occupied part of Germany."

The general beckoned Klügmann to one of his windows overlooking a courtyard.

"See this car and its driver down there?" he asked, pointing at a modest DKW limousine known for its robust but small two-stroke engine. "This is your service car. The driver will take you home to Lindau now. *Bon voyage!*"

Klügmann and Schmidt were already out the door when Gen. Koenig called them back.

"I need your help in another matter. We have appointed a nice man with good anti-Nazi credentials as Lindau County's chief executive. But he is a bit of a simpleton and knows nothing about administration and the law. He needs a legal advisor, but we haven't found one yet. If you can think of a good lawyer who wasn't a Nazi, please let me know."

"I'll see what I can do, General," Dr. Klügmann promised. With that, he and Paul Schmidt returned to Lindau in their sputtering new DKW.

Our train was about to enter Kassel central station when the steward returned to our compartment with sandwiches and mineral water, none of which Vati had ordered.

"Just a little snack to say goodbye, Herr Doktor," he said. "This train has reached its destination. I'll leave you now. But you are sitting in a through carriage, which will be hitched to an express train to Hamburg that has no diner."

It was getting dark as we continued our journey north into the British zone of occupation, an eerie trip through apparently lifeless cities such as Hanover that seemed to be made up of ruins only. Late at night, we arrived at Hamburg *Hauptbahnhof*. Dr. Klügmann was waiting for us on the platform and guided us to his car: A DKW with license plates bearing the initials "FB" (French Baden), indicating that it was registered in the former grand duchy of Baden, which now belonged to the French zone.

We drove through the blacked-out city that used to be—and is again—Germany's most elegant. There were no streetlights and no lit apartment buildings, not because Hamburg feared new air raids, but because they were wiped out in the war that was now over. More than half of its 414,000 dwellings had vanished in the firestorms whipped up by the lethal work of British and American bombers.

I would see much of the destruction in the following few days. It was worse than anything I had seen in Leipzig or Ulm. For now, I could only make out the eerie contours of a veritable sea of ruins through which the DKW was puttering.

The Alster River flows into a large lake in the center of Germany's second-largest municipality. I discovered the next morning that it was frozen over, allowing people to walk across it from one part of town to another, pulling sleighs. This lake was lined on one side by mid-nineteenth-century villas, all of which had survived undamaged. One of the most beautiful, Harvestehuder Weg 24, had belonged to the Klügmann clan since it was built as a sumptuous weekend home in 1840.

There, Dr. Klügmann's wife Marianne, whom I would call Omi from that evening on, gave me a plate of pea soup with a park sausage and bundled me off to a small bedroom. She was a funny, strict, and sharp-tongued lady, that Omi Klügmann, much like my real Omi in Leipzig. I saw much of her in the days before our departure on Epiphany 1948 while my father and Dr. Klügmann were locked in the latter's smoking room for mysterious discussions.

CHAPTER 2

Picnic, Poetry, and the English Major

SCHLOSS HAMBORN LIES LESS than five miles south of the ancient city of Paderborn, and Paderborn a mere 250 miles southwest of Hamburg. But on that Epiphany Day in 1948, less than three years after the end of World War II, the train journey there seemed very long.

There was no direct rail connection between the two cities. There still isn't. However, today's all-electric trains are twice as fast as the *Schnellzug* (fast express train) from Hamburg to Hanover in 1948 and the slower regional *Eilzug* from Hanover to Paderborn. Both had steam locomotives.

Neither had a dining car, so Omi Klügmann prepared us a food basket from the ample provisions supplied to her by a friendly farmer in a village near Lindau. She packed ham and liverwurst sandwiches, eggs, apples, Christmas cookies, mineral water, and a bottle of fruit brandy from the Lake Constance region for Vati. She arranged with the *Bahnhofsmission* (railway mission) in Hanover to meet us at our carriage from Hamburg, make us comfortable in the mission's well-heated hut on the platform, and then take us to the next train to Paderborn.

Schloß Hamborn in Eastern Westphalia, a boarding school, was the author's home for four years after his flight from the Soviet zone of occupation.

We traveled first class because, as a wounded veteran, Vati only had to pay the second-class fare for himself, while I traveled for free as his caregiver. He smiled as we left Hamburg; I had never seen him smile like that, at least not that early in the day.

"You seem in a jolly mood, Vati," I said.

"You are very perceptive. Yes, I am happy because I now know where I will live for the rest of my life."

"Good! Where?"

"In Lindau."

"Where will you stay?"

"With the Klügmanns. They invited me to stay with them in their summer home until they have found an apartment for me."

"What will you do?" I asked him.

"Remember what I told you on the train journey to Hamburg about Dr. Klügmann's meeting with Gen. Koenig in Baden-Baden? The General had asked Karl to find him a legal advisor for the chief executive of Lindau County. I'll be that advisor. And guess whose idea that was?"

"Tell me."

"Annemarie."

"The daughter with the lame arm?"

"Yes. We are both looking forward to this. Annemarie's marriage with Paul Schmidt is falling apart, and I have had no female company for a long time.

"That will soon be two Klügmann girls down with a third in the wings," I mocked him. "Who will the third one be?"

"There is no third Klügmann girl, you cheeky imp. If I could find your face, I would cuff you now; you are as loud-mouthed as your Omi," Vati said, laughing grimly.

My insolent jest soon proved prophetic. The romance between my father and Annemarie Schmidt née Klügmann cooled down soon enough. But in the summer, Annemarie's brother Peter arrived in

Lindau. He had been a first lieutenant and lost one leg and a buttock in combat. So severe were his injuries that he had to spend three years in hospital.

A tall and very beautiful young woman accompanied Peter. Uschi was her name. Peter announced that he would like to marry Uschi after graduating from Hamburg University (where he was studying law) if his parents gave the couple their blessing, which they did. Vati was smitten by Uschi's crisp accent; she hailed from Flensburg on the Danish border, Germany's northernmost city.

Uschi took stock of the sun-tanned blind veteran and liked what she saw. Alright, so he was already 51 years old, but he didn't look it. He seemed fit and, equally importantly, was a Herr Doktor.

"Your father seemed the perfect match for my sister Helga," Uschi told me decades later. Helga had been a naval intelligence officer and was much older than Uschi. She might have been 35 then, but unattached women of that wonderful age group stood little chance of finding compatible men in those days. They were either dead or in POW camps.

When Peter Klügmann and Uschi returned to Hamburg, she lost no time telling Helga about the blind but glamorous World War I hero she had met in Lindau. Helga, in turn, lost no time rushing to Lindau to meet Vati. The two almost immediately entered a "probationary marriage," as my father called it. The union was to be reviewed after six months.

It didn't last long, but long enough to let Marc-André Klügmann, Uschi's and Peter's son, tell me shortly before his premature death a few years ago, "Uwe, as the son of a man who had loved three of my aunts, you are definitely a member of our family." I was glad to hear that.

After this detour, I must now return to the train journey to my boarding school. Our *Eilzug* sauntered through snow-covered plains and hilly landscapes with pristine villages and small towns seemingly untouched by the war. Two British officers joined us in our compartment at one of the stops between Hanover and Paderborn. One was a major, the other a captain. Both laughed with us.

"Your laughter is so infectious! It is so rare to see merry Germans these days," explained the major in flawless German while staring happily out of the window.

"Enjoy this sight, young man," he said to me, "I always do when I travel through here before the train enters Paderborn, a city founded by Charlemagne. We wiped it out entirely, especially with an air raid only six weeks before Germany surrendered. I am so embarrassed looking at the ruins of what must have been such a beautiful town. We infantrymen have not fought this war to wipe out 1,100 years of Christian history but, on the contrary, to defend this legacy against barbarians."

"You are generous," my father suddenly said in English, "Alas, we Germans inflicted these barbarians on Europe by voting for them in 1933."

"Your English is very good. Where did you learn it?" the major asked.

"First at high school, of course, and then listening to the BBC three times a day."

"Was that not dangerous?" asked the younger officer.

"Of course, it was dangerous," Vati replied, shrugging his shoulders, "It was particularly dangerous for me, a senior civil servant who risked being sent to the guillotine for listening to enemy broadcasts and talking about them," said my father. "Still, I had to take my chances if I wanted to be told the truth."

He quickly changed the subject. "Gentlemen, I am hungry. Our friends in Hamburg have prepared a picnic for us. My son told me that we have great delicacies from southern Germany in our picnic

While at school in Schloß Hamburg, the author was in love with Helga Hopff, his pretty classmate. But he was too shy to tell her. So, with a few chalk strokes, he described his dream of embracing her and kept the picture to himself. Helga later became a renowned opera singer.

basket, including a little bottle of fruit spirit from Lake Constance. Please join us."

"May we contribute some whisky?" asked the major. "We are carrying several full hip flasks with us. I suggest we begin our meal with a *schluck* (gulp) of Scotch and end it with your fruit brandy."

My father smiled. Years later, he told me, "Meeting these two British officers was one of my most memorable experiences in the postwar years." Vati was an incorrigible Anglophile.

For his part, the major displayed an astonishing passion for Germany's distant past, especially for the part of the country we were traveling. He told us that he was a history teacher in civilian life while the young captain was a career officer.

"I wrote my doctoral dissertation about the poetry of the pre-Christian era," he explained, reciting, to my father's delight and in perfect meter, the oldest known text composed in Old High German, the 1,200-year-old *Hildebrandslied* (Song of Hildebrand):

> *Ik gihorta ðat seggen ðat sih urhettun*
> *ænon muotin Hiltibrant enti Haðubrant*
> *untar heriun tuem sunufatarungo*
> *iro saro rihtun garutun se iro guðhamun*
> *gurtun sih iro suert ana helidos ubar hringa*
> *do sie to dero hiltiu ritun.*

> I heard tell that warriors met
> in single combat Hildebrand and Hadubrand
> between two armies, son and father
> prepared their armor made ready their battle garments

girded on their swords the warriors, over their ring mail
when they rode to battle.

Today, I am sure that listening to this major quoting the
Hildebrandslied on the slow train to Paderborn made me fall in love
with alliterations, one of the loveliest features of both the German
and the English languages.

Hiltibrant enti Haðubrant / untar heriun tuem

All my life since, I've had this line in my head and suspect that
partly because of this, I developed a passion for composing tabloid
headlines, which also frequently consist of the "conspicuous rep-
etition of identical initial consonant sounds," as academics like to,
rather woodenly, define alliterations.

We were approaching Paderborn. "Don't look out of the window,"
the major advised me.

Of course, I did. What I saw out there was as terrifying as what
I had seen in Hamburg. I could not make out a single building that
hadn't burned down or at least been seriously damaged.

"Most of this happened on the 27th of March 1945, six weeks before
the war was over. During this air raid, 85 percent of the houses in central Paderborn were wiped out," the major said.

"How many people died?" I wanted to know.

"'Only' 900. I say the word 'only' in quotation marks because the
casualty rate would have been much higher had not most of the people of Paderborn fled into the countryside."

At Paderborn's *Hauptbahnhof* (central station), the two Englishmen
helped us carry our luggage to the platform where Uncle Fritz was
waiting for us. I had never met Uncle Fritz before and have never seen

him since. He was a cheerful man, one of Vati's first cousins in Lage, a town littered with descendants of "Red Moritz," who, in the days of the monarchy, was the opposition leader in the parliament of the principality of Lippe.

"Red Moritz," so-called because of his flaming red hair, had 13 children and left each of them a thriving business. My paternal grandmother Annemarie and her husband, Karl, inherited a still, which burned down because their drunken coachman had fallen asleep in the hayloft with his pipe still lit (q.v., *Urchin Trilogy*, Vol. I—*Urchin at War*), thus forcing his boss to rebuild his fortunes in the thriving kingdom of Saxony.

To Uncle Fritz, by contrast, the Moritz family's patriarch left a sober furniture factory that thrived in World War II, defying its nightmares. A stunning piece of evidence for Fritz' wealth was parked outside the bombed-out rump of the station. It was a dark-green Opel Kapitän.

Vati could not see this fancy vehicle, of course, but taking his seat behind Uncle Fritz's wife, he sensed that this automobile, belonging to the top of the line of General Motors' German subsidiary, must be very luxurious.

"Phew, this car feels comfortable," said Vati as we drove through Paderborn, hardly noticing its potholes, "how old is it?"

"Nine years, but in actual fact, it is as good as new. I hid it from the Wehrmacht during the war, covered up under straw in a friendly farmer's barn."

"But it must have been registered somewhere. How come the Wehrmacht didn't come after you?"

"There were ways to make the registration unhappen," Uncle Fritz answered without revealing details. He laughed loudly.

We passed a yellow streetcar with a sign indicating Detmold as its destination.

"Vati, here is a tram going to Detmold," I exclaimed carelessly. His face darkened. I could have kicked myself because I knew it was in Detmold where the British had offered him a senior position in the regional government of eastern Westphalia, a chance he passed on when Mutti refused to come back to him and reconstitute their marriage.

"Let's not talk about this anymore, Uwe," he said softly. "This topic is very hurtful to me."

Uncle Fritz made his Opel Kapitän crawl on the snow-covered road to Schloß Hamborn. Not that there was any other traffic; we encountered not a single vehicle. "One must drive very carefully here," he explained. "This snow hides extremely deep potholes, the legacy of very heavy combat right to the end of the war."

We passed the wreck of a German Tiger Tank, and another, and another.

"I bet there are many more hidden by these beech trees," he said as we passed the edge of a forest. "You must be careful playing here. There is also a lot of ammunition around, and not just that. A few weeks ago, I read that deep in the forest, children discovered a burned-out tank still containing the charred bodies of its crew."

He turned off the road and drove up a steep hill. "Here we are," he said with a sigh of relief as he turned left into the courtyard of a small castle with a big tower and a small turret.

"This is Schloß Hamborn. It once belonged to the family of Baroness Annette von Droste Hülshoff, the nineteenth-century poetess, novelist, and composer."

In the 19th century, Schloß Hamborn belonged
to the family of the beloved poetess, novelist and
composer, Baroness Annette von Droste-Hülshoff
(1797-1849). The castle was one if her many
residences in Westphalia. The author often sat in
the clearing where she used to read and rhyme.

At that moment, a slender gentleman appeared at the castle's por-
tico. I could not take my eyes off him because his head fit Omi's
description of members of the high Saxon aristocracy she had met at
the royal court in Dresden: His forehead was disproportionately high
and seemingly bigger than his face with its very sharp features, and a
strong, big nose.

"You must be Uwe," he said. "I am Georg-Moritz von Altenburg. We have been expecting you. Your mother announced your arrival."

"My mother?"

"Yes, I received a letter from her."

I looked at Vati. He said nothing but just stood there with a thin-lipped smile.

Herr von Altenburg shook Vati's hand, saying, "In her letter, your wife informed me that we had family connections. Evidently, her uncle was the resident advocate at our court."

"Your family's court?" my father asked him. "Who is your family?"

"I am Georg-Moritz, *Erbprinz* (prince-heir) of the grand duchy of Saxony-Altenburg. If Germany were still a monarchy, I would be the reigning grand duke."

Realizing that he was in the presence of a member of the ancient dynasty that had spawned the elector Frederick the Wise, Luther's protector (not to mention the royal family of his beloved England), Vati asked him with unusual softness, "Your Highness, how are you connected with Hamborn?"

"Please, just call me Herr von Altenburg," the prince replied. "I don't use my title while Germany is still occupied. Our British rulers wouldn't like it. Anyway, I am one of the founders of this institution. Before the war, I ran our organic farm."

"And during the war?"

"This institution started out as a home for mentally handicapped children. During the war, I tried to save them from the National Socialists' euthanasia program. But then the Gestapo arrested me and took me into what they called *Schutzhaft* (protective custody),' in other words, they threw me into a concentration camp."

"Forgive me this interruption, Herr von Altenburg, but we must leave very soon," Uncle Fritz suddenly said. "I am Dr. Siemon's cousin. I live in Lage, where Dr. Siemon was born and where my entire family is looking forward to seeing him again after many years. Lage is not far, but I want to get us home before dark. The road has dangerous potholes hidden under the snow and invisible at night."

"You are right! The roads all around us are perilous. Please allow Dr. Siemon to sign a few papers in our office quickly, and you'll be on your way. Meanwhile, I shall call the lady in charge of Uwe's dorm over there in the *Kavaliershaus* (gentlemen's annex) where all our pupils live. There is no room for them here in the castle at the moment because it has been taken over by nuns running a Catholic retirement home."

The lady's name was Fräulein Boy. I found her very appealing as she guided me across the castle's lawn to the Tudor-style *Kavaliershaus*. Uncle Fritz clearly liked her too, for he eagerly followed us, carrying my suitcase and staring at her derrière.

I instinctively realized that a brief, warm interlude in my otherwise complicated relationship with Vati had ended. In the school office, I had embraced him, trying not to shed a tear in the presence of strangers. He said, "I will try to have you come to Lindau during your summer break, *mein Junge* (my boy). That's a promise."

And then I entered a strange new world, a world inhabited by nobles, nuns, and nutcases. It was a space filled with children believing falsely that something was wrong with them because, in the war and its immediate aftermath, they had witnessed the horrors of a manifestly broken world.

Musiker

im

Jahr.

The author's favorite pastime was drawing
amusing scenes in some sparse charcoal strokes.
The series titles, "Musiker im Jahr" he drew while
studying at boarding school as a Christmas
present for his mother. He was then 12 years old.

Not only in his caricatures, but also in his watercolors, the author presented his objects in clear sharp lines, as in the winter scene he painted of the beech trees near Schloß Hamborn. "I see my world in clear contours while playing with the nuances in my head," he says. " By contrast, Anthroposophic art, on the other hand, reminds me all too often of a multi-colored fruit soup that has spilled over." His art teacher at the Rudolf-Steiner-Schule in Wuppertal interpreted Uwe's work as evidence of a disturbed and furious young mind and sent one of his drawings as a product of a demented astral body to the Goetheanum near Baqsel in Switzerland, the Steinerians' Vatican, as it where. The author, on the other hand, just had some good fun.

CHAPTER 3

Among Nobles, Nuns, and Nutcases

MUTTI KEPT HER PROMISE. Late in the Lenten season, she again took the risk of crossing the border between the Soviet and the British zones of occupation without a Russian exit visa. Of course, she came to Schloß Hamborn primarily to visit me, but she also had two ulterior motives: One was to give a concert, for which I was grateful because I loved to hear her sing; the other reason was to persuade Prince Georg-Moritz to marry her.

She took long walks with the Hereditary Prince Georg-Moritz under the beech and oak trees in the woods around Schloß Hamborn, trying to persuade him that at the age of almost 48 years, it was time for him to get married and brazenly offering herself as bride. Before returning to Leipzig, she informed me with tears in her eyes that he had rejected her advances, saying,

"*Ach, gnädige Frau, dafür bin ich zu degeneriert* (Ah, gracious lady, I am too degenerate for that)."

I teased her, "What a shame! It would have been so nice to be able to say, 'my mother, the princess,' or, if Germany ever became a monarchy again, 'my mother, the grand duchess!'"

She stared at me, hurt. Omi's blunt comment on this new episode of her daughter's pretentiousness brought her to tears: "Ruth!" Omi had said sternly, as so often before, "you do have a fart in your head!"

Come to think of it, though, Mutti would have been a good fit in Hamborn, where "everybody around here seems nuts, including us children," according to Klaus Harlan, the senior of *Ulmenzimmer* (elm tree room), my dorm. He was two years older than I and a brilliant musician who owned a vast array of recorders ranging from a huge great bass instrument to a tiny piccolo device, the latter carved from ivory.

"What do you expect?" Klaus went on, "Most of us have gone through hell in the war and its aftermath. Some of us had their parents killed by the Nazis. Others are the offspring of Nazis; for example, the father of a girl in your class is a general imprisoned for war crimes in Italy. Still others have lived through the horrors of the expulsion of millions from Germany's eastern territories, such as East and West Prussia, Pomerania, and Silesia. Bear that in mind, Uwe, as you are wondering about the strange characters in your class and in this dorm," said Klaus, whose own family reflected the fault line of our defeated nation. He belonged to the Harlans, a dynasty of famous instrument makers from Markneukirchen in Saxony, whereas his Uncle Veit had infamously produced an anti-Semitic film much beloved by Hitler.

If we children had one thing in common, it was hunger, an ever-present sensation dominating our daily lives, causing intense physical pain, and diminishing our ability to study. This wasn't the school's fault. The British military government allowed civilians in its zone of occupation 1,200 calories per day and had temporarily confiscated our 650-acre farm that could have fed all of us.

In the ten o'clock break on my first day in Schloß Hamborn, we children were given two slices of black bread with a revolting spread, which turned out to be the previous night's thickened pea soup. There was no butter. Neither was there any ham, luncheon meat, or cheese. We had to make do with some sour-tasting gunk.

Starvation warped our characters and made us do reprehensible, revolting, or crazy things we would not have done otherwise. We stole from the food parcels the few sons of rich Ruhr industrialists in our dorms received from home. One roommate, the scion of an ancient but impoverished noble family, sought to harvest a nutritional supplement from his nose. The young baron—whom we nicknamed *Wöbbel*—attached his daily pickings meticulously in a straight line on the metal frame of his bunk bed. Sunday mornings, before Chapel, was harvest time. *Wöbbel* ate the previous week's entire yield. We others watched him with revulsion but said nothing, all too aware of our own imperfections.

One boy displayed an idiosyncrasy that humored all of us. For weeks, we had noticed that every time we returned from breakfast, another chunk of wood had been gnawed out of the back rests of the eight chairs in our room. We also saw two candles on our long table growing shorter, not from above, but from below. I also remarked that "*Schnifi*," whose real name was Gerhard Fischer, never joined us for breakfast.

Schnifi was a hilarious oddball. He came to us from Shanghai, where he and his family had spent the last war years in an internment camp but were well-fed. *Schnifi* was very taciturn, which made us speculate that his Chinese might have been better than his German. It occurred to us that his eyes seemed somewhat slanted, although he was clearly a young, blond German.

One morning, three of our roommates decided to solve this riddle and catch the chair and candle aficionado. We left the breakfast table early and tiptoed into the *Ulmenzimmer* to be treated to an unforgettable spectacle of *Schnifi* chomping away at a chair while holding a candle in his right hand for his second course.

We burst out laughing, whereupon Schnifi spun around and explained to us with a thin smile, "*Ich esse lieber Kistenholz, als dass ich deren salzige Morgensuppe fresse.*" (I'd rather eat box wood than their salty morning soup).

He was referring to the sickening oatmeal slurry we were fed every morning—sickening because it was rendered unpalatable by the absence of milk and sugar, none of which was available in sufficient amounts to nourish a horde of children.

Schnifi might have been an amiable crank at boarding school, but he was also a loner who one day disappeared without leaving a forwarding address or ever contacting any of his roommates again. Decades later we learned he was a successful naval architect.

All of us turned out quite well in adulthood. Klaus Harlan became a celebrated composer. Another boy, Jobst Ferdinand von Strantz, a young baron with a zany sense of humor, rose to be chief administrator of a German imperial family's assets. In the *Ulmenzimmer*, Jobst competed with Christfried, an effeminate roommate, in humoring us after evening prayers, trying to make us forget our growling stomachs.

Christfried intoned an Indian prayer, "Aum, aum," thus mocking the syncretistic anthroposophists among the grownups on campus. We were bemused by the way they wafted through Hamborn's muddy paths with an air of spiritual superiority, their eyes affixed on the unseen Ground of Being, describing to us the essence of the human species: We were not just a finite lump of cells, for we also possessed an immortal astral body which, after the former's death, would transfer to a new incarnation, but not before suffering for misdeeds committed in one's terrestrial existence. This pain must be endured in *Karmaloca*, the space where astral bodies are parked in the interim period.

"Aum," hummed Christfried, "worship me!"

"Aum," we responded, "but Christfried, whom are we worshiping?"

"Aum," Christfried answered, allowing his nightshirt to slide from his shoulders. "I am Frau Buddha. You must worship me."

"Aum," we chimed, but I objected: "Christfried, Buddha was a monk. He had no wife."

"Aum," said he, "look at me. I am living proof that Buddha is married. Look at me. I am his wife! Aum, aum, aum."

"Aum, aum," we mumbled over and over again until we fell asleep, forgetting our growling stomachs.

I best remember Christfried, who later became a dress designer, by the splendid one-liner he crafted when refusing our plea to join the "Blue Flame Society." In our struggle against starvation, we had discovered that our school's kitchen was storing victuals in the basement of the *Kavalierhaus* where we lived. The cellar was locked, but eventually, we managed to break into it. What did we find? Nothing but large onions!

We helped ourselves to some, ate them greedily, and realized that a certain number of onions, though not nourishing, would generate massive flatulence. We German boys, being by definition anal, found this discovery thrilling.

I believe it was Jobst von Strantz, the future trustee of the Hohenzollern dynasty's possessions, who informed us that if we set light to such a wind, it would turn into a beautiful blue flame.

So, most of us agreed that every Friday, one of us was to be chosen by lot to sneak into the cellar, steal three big onions, devour them at top speed after supper, and then wait, naked, for the desired result. As the expected storm grew inside him to an explosion, the chosen one would stretch out, belly first, on the table. We lit what was left of a candle after Schnifi had had his way with it. "Now!" shouted the onion eater. We turned off the light and held the candle to his anus, and, *pfft!* Out shot a brilliant blue flame.

"Man, there goes your astral body on its way to Karmaloca," jested Christfried, a.k.a Frau Buddha.

"Aum," we yelled, laughing. "Why don't you produce a blue flame next Friday?" Shaking his head, Christfried coined his most glorious bon mot:

"Frau Buddha does not fart."

That said, "Frau Buddha" participated enthusiastically in a prank directed at the Sisters of St. Vincent de Paul, who ran a Catholic retirement home occupying most of the actual castle of the Schloß Hamborn estate. This retirement home was originally in Paderborn but burned down in a devastating air raid only days before the end of World War II.

We were told that the British were embarrassed when they discovered what RAF planes had done to this venerable Christian institution. So, they vowed to rebuild it quickly and moved its residents temporarily to Hamborn. We children found this reasonable enough but found the sisters unfriendly, presumably because anthroposophy was anathema to their Catholic faith.

The nuns never returned our greetings nor smiled at us as if we children had invented the Karmaloca philosophy, which most of us found nutty. So, the boys of *Ulmenzimmer* pondered how we could teach them a lesson.

"Is it true that under their pointed white hoods, the Sisters of St. Vincent are bald?" asked Jobst.

"Let's find out!" I suggested.

"How?"

"We could knock the hoods off their heads with snowballs or lumps of clay."

"How?"

There was a bunker between the Schloß and our dorm. It was one of the remnants of the war, like so many of its vestiges all around us: burned-out tanks, trucks, and other martial paraphernalia. We knew that the sisters stored their vegetables there. We observed them walking in and out of the bunker, which had several air shafts.

"That's where we will catch them," said I. "Do any of you have a flashlight?"

"I do," said Frau Buddha, giggling fiendishly.

"When we see a nun enter the bunker, we must position ourselves strategically. Two or three of you will stand close to the exit. I'll have a stock of snowballs and mud lumps ready. Frau Buddha and I will kneel by an air shaft. As soon as Frau Buddha's flashlight illuminates a white hood down there in the bunker, I will try to shoot it off the nun's head with my snow and clay. Then we will find out if she has any hair or not."

To some extent, our plan worked. My snowball and lumps of clay hit their target. Sadly, the nun's headgear remained in place. Screaming, she came running out of the bunker, immediately identified me as the culprit, grabbed me by my right ear, and dragged me to Siegfried Pickert, the headmaster. In her anger, she failed to lock the bunker door, thus allowing my roommates to steal respectable amounts of carrots, peas, and beans.

Herr Pickert, a leading anthroposophist and opponent of the Nazi regime, was also our beloved Latin and Greek teacher. He pretended to look hurt while listening to the nun's prosecutorial charge against me. As he sentenced me to stand behind my chair at lunch and dinner for an entire week, I detected a twitch in the corners of his mouth. When I paid him a visit at Schloß Hamborn ten years before he died at the age of 103, he said,

"Uwe, what you did to that nun was one of the funniest pranks I have witnessed in my many years as headmaster."

Siegfried Pickert, headmaster of Schloß Hamborn and the author's Greek and Latin teacher. He lived to the age of 103.

Siegfried Pickert before he died.

CHAPTER 4

Non-Dogmas,
Mercilessly Enforced

ANTHROPOSOPHY IS A WORLDVIEW rooted in 19th-century
German idealism and mysticism. One might call it a harbinger of
today's New Age movement, which also has a sinister progenitor:
the English occultist Aleister Crowley (1875–1947), who called himself
"the evilest man on earth." His mantra, "Do as thou wilt shall be the
whole of the Law," adorned the first web page of the Church of Satan
for a long time. The American LSD guru Timothy Leary, who pronounced himself as Crowley's successor, abridged this slogan to "Do
your own thing," the catchphrase of New Age.

I am not saying that my anthroposophical teachers in Schloß
Hamborn were evil—quite to the contrary. I owe most of them enor-
mous gratitude for their love and skill in guiding us through dire
times, even though their philosophy seemed alien to me. Their fusion
of Christian thought with Hindu / Buddhist beliefs, especially the
notion Karmaloca, the space in which man's astral body must suffer
for his misdeeds in the last life before being reincarnated, was just
incompatible with the Gospel my Lutheran Omi had taught me so

convincingly in our Leipzig air raid shelter: "Your sins are forgiven by God's grace through your faith in Christ's atoning death for you and me on the Cross."

That said, anthroposophy and Aleister Crowley's New Age share common roots. Both harken back to the 19th-century Spiritism of French schoolteacher Hippolyte Léon Denizard Rivail (1804–1869), better known by his pen name Allan Kardech, who claimed that souls in transit from one incarnation to the next can be called upon for counsel.

Kardech considered himself a Christian, as does anthroposophy's religious appendage called Christian Community (in German, *Christengemeinschaft*). Blending Western and Eastern faiths, this church body claims to have no dogma. Yet in Schloß Hamborn, where it was and still is the predominant faith group, I found out how sternly non-dogmas can be enforced.

One of its tenets willed that we must never kick anybody or anything with our feet—neither somebody's rear nor a leather globule. This meant that football (soccer), the world's most beloved sport, was banned from campus.

This did not sit well with the boys in the dorms on my floor. Forbidding soccer to German kids struck us as particularly idiotic. Countermeasures were in order. So, we converted the corridor in our dorm into a soccer field. The window on the south side of the hallway served as one goal. We kept it open lest we smash the glass. If the goalie failed to catch a ball, he had to run outside, down one flight of stairs, and halfway around the building to retrieve it before dogmatic anti-dogmatists could confiscate it.

The opposite goal was the door to Herbert Weiß' apartment, a fitting venue. Herr Weiß was a choleric little man we loved and loathed.

On the one hand, he was a dazzling music teacher with a knack for making us understand the structure of the fugue, the sonata, and its larger sister, the symphony. He was also our religion instructor and conducted Sunday services called "Acts." In this capacity, he pronounced soccer as "offensive to the Higher Worlds," a blatant nonsense.

One day, I was the center forward of my team and scored five successive goals against Herr Weiß's door: *wrrumph, wrrumph, wrrumph, wrrumph, wrrumph.* He stormed out of his apartment, the picture of fury: his pitch-black hair flopping wildly around his contorted red physiognomy. He instantly identified me as the culprit and boxed my left ear with such force that it went deaf for six weeks, an odd thing to do for a music teacher whose ground rule should have been to protect his students' hearing from harm.

My moment of taking revenge came a few days later when Herr Weiß made us pupils compose a fugue each in class. I completed my assignment but kept the scoresheet to myself at first; in its place, I handed Herr Weiß the caricature of a disgruntled man with a crumpled floppy hat angrily kicking a ball (see nearby drawing), thus violating not only his bias against soccer but also the anthroposophists' dislike of clear lines in the arts. They prefer colors flowing freely into each other, ruling out the satirical drawings that were my forte.

Enraged by my insolence, Herr Weiß rushed towards me, intent on boxing my other ear, the right one this time. My classmates saved me and my ear by pounding their desks furiously, prompting Herr Weiß to retreat to his piano.

To be fair to the Hamborn faculty, most were not violent. Some teachers were lovable even though we teased them relentlessly.

Infuriated by the ideologically motivated prohibition
to play soccer, the author drew the caricature of an
angry footballer and handed it in to his music teacher
in lieu of a fugue he was assigned to write.

Prince Georg-Moritz was one of those. He taught history, a perfect subject for the scion of the 1,000-year-old House of Wettin, one of the oldest dynasties in Europe, of which the British royal family is part, although it took the name of Windsor in an anti-German tiff in World War I.

One day, I sneaked a stinkhorn into the prince's briefcase—stinkhorns are penis-shaped morels that grow amply in the woods around Schloß Hamborn, emitting vile and long-lasting smells. The prince reacted in a way one would expect of a nobleman: he ignored the prank, obliging us pupils to follow his example, suffering the odors silently while following him on his journey back to the Holy Roman Empire of the German Nation, an era when his ancestors elected the Kaiser. This was the First Reich, which all of us wished had never been succeeded by the second, under the two Kaisers Wilhelm I and II, and then by Hitler's murderous Third Reich.[1]

On the other hand, our French teacher, Sonja Ziemann, responded much less nobly to tomfooleries: she whined. She was perhaps the most useless of our instructors, much to my regret because I had loved the French language since learning it in my early childhood on the lap of my nanny Raymonde from Amiens. Fräulein (Miss) Ziemann lived in a room above the stables where the school's two horses were housed. Incongruously, they were named Liese and Lotte, even though they were geldings. Their minder was Count Wolfgang von Gahlen, everybody's favorite character on campus.

Wolfgang was a slightly retarded Westphalian nobleman whom the Nazis would have liquidated in their euthanasia campaign

---

1 The Second Reich was the brief reign of the Hohenzollern Kaisers, Wilhelm I, Friedrich, and Wilhelm II (1871–1918).

against "*lebensunwürdiges Leben*" (life unworthy of living)[2] had not the anthroposophists protected him. We loved Wolfgang for his hilarious quips, which we were never sure were intentionally comical or simply products of a feeble mind. Once, during a performance of Gershwin's *Rhapsody in Blue* and Ravel's *Boléro* in the Paderborn concert hall, we noticed that he had plonked himself in the front row.

"Wolfgang," we asked him on our way home in a horse cart pulled by Liese and Lotte, "Why did you sit there? Don't you know that the acoustics are much better in the middle of the hall?"

"I know that," answered Wolfgang with a broad grin, "but the closer I sit to the stage, the better I see the water dripping out of the trumpets."

We laughed and hugged him.

Back to Fräulein Ziemann, Wolfgang's neighbor. She had an extraordinary knack for turning French into the dreariest subject taught at Schloß Hamborn.

"Why don't you make us read Molière?" I asked her one day in class, having read with delight this 18th-century French playwright's hilarious work, *Le Bourgeois Gentilhomme* (The Bourgeois Nobleman), in German a few years earlier under my mother's guidance.

"School is not a comic theater," she insisted inanely. This called for punishment.

So, one day before class, we roped Fräulein's door handle from the outside, making it impossible for her to leave her room. Then, we waited silently in our classroom. As we expected, she didn't show up

---

2 Wolfgang was a relative of Clemens August Count von Gahlen, the Roman Catholic bishop of Münster, whose powerful sermons against the Nazi euthanasia program ultimately compelled the regime of the Third Reich to stop the wanton mass murder of mentally disabled children. Von Gahlen later became a cardinal.

because she couldn't. After 20 minutes, we went to the headmaster's office and feigned concern: "Is Fräulein Ziemann alright? We are worried! She didn't come to teach us French."

Herr Pickert sent out a search team to scour unsuccessfully the nearby woods. In the end, one of the boys had the brilliant idea to check her room: "Perhaps she is sick, perhaps even dead," he said. The search team unbound Fräulein Ziemann's doorhandle and found her in tears, sitting on her unmade bed, howling that she would not teach our class again: not now, not ever!

She was done with these malignant twelve-year-olds, period!

To our delight, she kept her word. Children are mean. When we met her in the park, we chanted, *Fessel-Fräulein, Fessel-Fräulein* (girl in ropes). During morning prayers, she stood as far from us as possible. She didn't last much longer in Schloß Hamborn, which was just fine with us.

Alas, Fräulein Ziemann was the only qualified French teacher at our school, where this language was a compulsory subject as of fifth grade, along with English, Latin, and Greek. Herr Pickert tasked Fräulein Elisabeth Rassmann, our beloved class teacher, to inflict her limited French vocables on us pupils. Recognizing her inadequacy in the language of Baudelaire, she made a life-changing decision.

Fräulein Rassmann was a refugee spinster from Silesia in her early fifties who took great pride in her virginal state, insisting on being called Fräulein (Miss) rather than Frau (Mrs.) Rassmann. An ex-Catholic, she wove her hair into what we children called *eine Glaubenszwiebel* (a faith bun) at the back of her head. She wore no makeup and kept her blouse buttoned all the way up to the top.

After teaching a few calamitous French lessons, Fräulein Rassmann took a sabbatical to improve her language skills at the Sorbonne University in Paris. When she returned six months later, her blouse was unbuttoned at the top, her *Glaubenszwiebel* flopped more loosely from the back of her head, and we detected a trace of rouge on her lips.

"You may now call me *Frau* Rassmann," she announced as she resumed charge of our class, prompting us to give her a standing ovation. Little by little, her story came out. In the City of Light, she had met a taxi driver who claimed to be—and probably was, too—a refugee prince from St. Petersburg; Paris was full of those blue-blooded Russian cabbies then. As I found out later in my adult life, there is no better locus for linguistic advancement than the loving arms of a member of the opposite sex. And so, not only did Frau Rassmann return from France equipped to share her love of French with us, but she also surprised us with her newly acquired passion for the Russian language, which she perfected a few years later during yet another sabbatical; this time in Moscow.

I shall return to this superb teacher later, but for now, I must resume my narrative about the Schloß Hamborn faculty.

Next to Frau Rassmann, our English teacher, Konrad Funke, was my preferred instructor. When we met, he had only recently been discharged from a British prisoner of war camp where he had worked as an interpreter. Herr Funke taught us the English language, culture, and humor so vividly that I developed a lasting love for them. That I now write books and sometimes satirical poems in English, that I wrote my M.A. thesis and my doctoral dissertation in English and got both published, that I dream in English, that I opted for London as my first foreign posting when I was a young reporter, indeed, that I have been happily married to an Englishwoman for almost 60 years by the time of this writing, all that I readily attribute to Konrad Funke's teaching skills.

He made me aware of what English and German have in common—not just countless words (hand = *Hand*; arm = *Arm*; finger = *Finger*; lips = *Lippen*; shoulder = *Schulter*; knee = *Knie*; foot = *Fuß*)—but also their meter, their frequent use of alliteration, and their endless possibilities for creating neologisms.

The first English poem Herr Funke taught us has remained in my head for over seven decades. It is by John Masefield (1878–1967), is titled "Sea Fever," and reads thus:

> I must go down to the seas again,
> to the lonely sea and the sky,
> And all I ask is a tall ship,
> and a star to steer her by,
> And the wheel's kick and the wind's song
> and the white sail's shaking,
> And a grey mist on the sea's face,
> and a gray dawn breaking.
>
> I must go down to the seas again,
> for the call of the running tide
> Is a wild call and a clear call
> that may not be denied,
> And all I ask is a windy day,
> with the white clouds flying,
> And the flung spray and the blown spume,
> and the seagulls crying.

I must go down to the seas again,
to the vagrant gypsy life,
To the gull's way and the whale's way
where the wind's like a whetted knife,
And all I ask is a merry yarn,
from a laughing fellow-rover
And quiet sleep and a sweet dream
when the long trick's over.

How I desired so much to visit this island nation Konrad Funke most beautifully described! To see the English cities, towns, and villages of which he showed us photographs, with their elite public schools (private boarding schools), such as Eaton and Harrow, which seemed far more elegant than Schloß Hamborn! How I yearned for the beauty of its monarchy, a blessing that we Germans were denied after World War I, as Omi, my maternal grandmother, told me sorrowfully every day when I was little!

Another reason I remember Konrad Funke fondly is that he was the father of my oldest friend, Hartmut. The two of us were—and still are—an odd match. Hartmut is a Prussian. As a child, he seemed introverted and taciturn, the opposite of me, the boisterous and loquacious Saxon. Moreover, he had bought into his parents' anthroposophical convictions while I was then, and still am, a committed Lutheran; our beliefs were incompatible.

Yet, we liked each other. We scrupulously avoided compromising our harmony with pointless bickering over religious issues as we explored the beech and oak woods around Hamborn, inspecting burned-out Tiger tanks and the remnants of howitzers and military encampments, residues of the recent war.

To bridge our divide, I founded a new religion and named it *Salmisekte* because the object of our worship was the *Salmiakpastille*, a small, diamond-shaped licorice pastille almost all German boys loved to suck. I consecrated myself as the sect's high priest and ordained Hartmut as my adjunct.

In Rudolf Steiner schools, not only are gardening, sewing, darning, and knitting courses compulsory, but also handicraft classes, which Hartmut and I shamelessly converted into production facilities for plywood amulets of our new faith. They were rhombus-shaped like the licorice pastilles. Two of them were large. I painted one in gold for myself and the other in silver for Hartmut. Then we made scores more jujus, though much smaller and colored black, for recruiting ordinary congregants.

One morning, we entered our respective classes—Hartmut was one grade lower than I—wearing our priestly insignia around our necks and chanting a liturgy I had adapted from my Omi's bogus Spiritist séances in World War II. "*Aum, Salmi, aum, aum, aum,*" we hummed.

"What is this supposed to mean?" Fräulein Rassmann asked me in front of my sniggering classmates.

"Aum, I am the High Priest of a new sect worshiping the *Salmiakpastille*," I answered. "*Aum, Salmi, aum!*"

This sounded sufficiently Oriental and, therefore, familiar to Fräulein Rassmann's now neo-anthroposophist ears, so she let it pass with a grin whilst my classmates were intrigued. After class, all of them signed up as new members. I handed each a licorice amulet exhorting them not to wear it until they had fulfilled their initiation obligation to steal at least two aluminum tins of *Salmiakpastillen* from the *Kaufhalle* shop in Paderborn, one for himself or herself, the other for the good of the congregation to be communally sucked in a rhombic liturgy.

When we met during the mid-morning break, Hartmut and I had enlisted 55 members to our sect. Two days later, we found ourselves in possession of 150 tins of Salmis because some zealous new congregants had stolen three or more of these tiny tins. Hartmut and I rewarded them by elevating them to the lower priesthood, chanting: Aum, Salmi, Aum!

We realized, of course, that *Salmiakpastillen* were of no salvific value—you can't suck your way to eternal bliss. Still, they had one praiseworthy quality in that they numbed our craving for food, which governed my first year in Schloß Hamborn, much to the detriment of my scholastic achievements.

We woke up with our stomachs growling. Our stomachs rumbled during class. The bland slices of brown bread we were fed, with its impalpable spread, during our morning break could not satisfy our indignant digestive systems. Fräulein Rassmann, our consummate class teacher, brought up the issue of famine at a faculty meeting, prompting Herr Pickert, our headmaster and Latin instructor, to remark:

"*Plenus venter non studet libenter* (a full belly does not study gladly)," prompting Fräulein Rassmann to create an unforgettable retort to this well-known proverb:

"*Sed neque ieiunus* (but neither does an empty belly)."

The next morning, she reported this exchange of Latin words in class, adding: "Children, the time has come for us to take action."

It so happened that Schloß Hamborn owned 750 acres of arable land but was not permitted to farm its fields or have children pilfer the apples, pears, and cherries in its orchard, for the British military government had confiscated this estate and entrusted it to a professional agronomist expelled from Germany's lost eastern territories in East Prussia.

In fairness to our victors, their decision, though cruel, made sense to us, given the anthroposophists' inefficient "biodynamic cultivation methods" our gardening teacher taught us: "Here is what you have to do if you want to grow tasty tomatoes," he proclaimed. "With your right middle finger, you dig seven holes in a neat circle into the ground and fill them with natural manure. Then, you burrow another hole into the precise center of this circle. Into this hole, you drop the tomato seeds and cover them with soil."

That evening in our dorm, we boys mocked this horticultural gobbledygook by chanting, to the tune of the German folk song, *Mein Hut, der hat drei Ecken* (my hat, it has three corners), "*Meine Frucht, die braucht acht Löcher*" (my fruit, it needs eight holes), for it was obvious to us that surrounding tomato seeds with seven holes filled with feces was no practical way to feed hundreds of hungry mouths.

The fiendish decision by the Royal Army captain overseeing agricultural activities in the rural district of Paderborn implied that we children were forbidden to eat even one single apple, cherry, or pear ripening in the orchard just across the dirt road below our dorm windows.

Fräulein Rassmann, ever the consummate teacher, used our plight to devise an interdisciplinary course in Christian ethics, chemistry, and economics.

"Children, what does the Seventh Commandment say?" she asked us one morning.

"Thou shalt not steal, Fräulein Rassmann," we answered in unison.

"Do you think this also applies to *Mundraub* (oral theft)?" she continued.

We squabbled: yes, no...well, theoretically, yes, it's theft because there are no footnotes under the Ten Commandments ... never mind that we are hungry, we must eat ... that's no excuse ... but the orchard belongs to Schloß Hamborn ... that doesn't count, the Tommies won the war, not us ... on the other hand, the anthroposophists were also persecuted by the Nazis ... the Tommies don't care, we just have to follow their law...

"Silence, children!" Fräulein Rassmann commanded. "There is a way out. Neither the Seventh Commandment nor common law cover *Fallobst* (fallen fruit).

"*Igitt* (yuck), Fräulein Rassmann. Fallen apples are rotten and have worms," interjected Editha, daughter of a land-owning noble family from Pomerania.

"Not every fallen apple is rotten and has worms, but even with brown spots and worms, it can serve a purpose: You might slip on it during your evening strolls through the orchard. You might fall against the trunk of a tree, causing ripe apples to drop to the ground and thus become *Fallobst*, and they are yours."

"But Fräulein Rassmann, we might be able to eat one or two apples, not ten or twenty. They would give us the runs," said one of the boys, not the brightest in our class.

"Indeed! That's why you must carry baskets on your evening walks through the orchard to collect *Fallobst*, should you find it."

"And then?"

"Then we juice the fallen fruit. As the juice ferments into cider, you will scour the woods for empty bottles left behind by Wehrmacht and

British units during the last battles of the war. I have seen plenty of bottles all over the place. You bring them back to our chemistry lab, where we will wash them in hot water. I have discovered a source for corks in Paderborn."

We children sensed that Fräulein Rassmann was planning something exciting but were clueless about what this ingenious woman had in mind. In the following days, the chemistry lab was filled with hundreds of empty bottles and jars of cider, the scent permeating the whole building.

"What are you kids doing? What is Fräulein Rassmann up to?" other teachers asked us. We shrugged our shoulders. Eventually, Fräulein Rassmann summoned our class to a nightly chemistry lesson. She taught us how to distill the cider into brandy and bottle it, an art she had learned in rural Silesia.

"What will we do with all that brandy, Fräulein Rassmann?" I asked her. "We can't drink it!"

"No, but you can sell it to the Tommies (British soldiers). In a fortnight, the British forces will conduct their annual maneuver in the Hamborn woods, and our Schloß-park will be transformed into a tent city. The Tommies are known to be heavy drinkers. So, after dark, you sneak into their tents, armed with bottles of apple brandy, and whisper, 'Psst, want some Schnapps?'"

"How much shall we charge them?"

"Two packs of Senior Service or Player's Navy Cut cigarettes per bottle."

"And what are we going to do with those cigarettes?"

"We sell them on the black market. Cigarettes are the only hard currency in Germany. One pack of Senior Service will buy you one kilo of smoked ham or 60 eggs. I want you children to attend my classes with a *plenus venter* (full belly).

The Tommies came and bought the booze, parting with many cartons of cigarettes.

One morning, Fräulein Rassmann announced: "*Ausflug* (excursion)! Get your rucksacks, children!" We filled the knapsacks with cartons of cigarettes and marched seven kilometers to the farmers' black market behind Paderborn's ancient cathedral, of which Fräulein Rassmann taught us: "Charlemagne commissioned the first church built at this space in the ninth century."

As we followed Fräulein Rassmann on the dusty road to Paderborn we sang:

> *Geh' aus, mein Herz, und suche Freud*
> *In dieser lieben Sommerzeit*
> *An Deines Gottes Gaben*
> *Schau an der schönen Gärten Zier*
> *Und siehe wie sie mir und Dir*
> *Sich ausgeschmücket haben*
> *Sich ausgeschmücket haben.*

This hymn by Paul Gerhardt (1607–1670) is such a charming reportage about the beauty of God's creation that I must inflict at least four of its 15 stanzas in English on my readers; they were translated by Catherine Winkworth (1827–1878):

> Go forth, my heart, and seek delight,
> While summer reigns so fair and bright,
> View God's abundance daily;

The beauty of these gardens see,
Behold how they for me and thee
Have decked themselves so gaily,
Have decked themselves so gaily.

The trees with spreading leaves are blessed,
The earth her dusty rind has dressed
In green so young and tender.
Narcissus and the tulip fair
Are clothed in raiment far more rare
Than Solomon in splendor,
Than Solomon in splendor.

The lark soars upward to the skies,
And from her cote the pigeon flies,
Her way to woodlands winging.
The silver-throated nightingale
Fills mountain, meadow, hill and dale
With her delightful singing,
With her delightful singing.

Thy mighty working, mighty God,
Wakes all my powers; I look abroad
And can no longer rest:
I, too must sing when all things sing,
And from my heart the praises ring
The Highest loveth best.
The Highest loveth best.

When we returned to Schloß Hamborn, we were laden with a wealth of meats, sausages, eggs, fruits, and vegetables, thanks to Fräulein Rassmann's Schnapps-cum-cigarette caper. Over 70 years on, I often think back to us seventh graders traipsing like baby chicks behind Fräulein Rassmann, our Mother Hen. I still see the faith bun on the back of her head bopping up and down to the rhythm of Paul Gerhardt's song and smile: This was my most memorable lesson in 13 years of primary and secondary schooling.

CHAPTER 5

An Urchin Divided

IN 1948, OUR SMALL family was spread over three locations in a divided Germany. I lived in the British zone of occupation in the northwestern part of the country, my father 400 miles south, in Lindau on the shores of Lake Constance, a French-occupied corner of Bavaria. Mutti was sealed off in Leipzig in the Soviet zone, 210 miles east of Schloß Hamborn. Some 350 miles separated Vati and Mutti, plus the Iron Curtain and tons of thick air.

Although I lived far away from my divorced parents, I was constantly exposed to the acrimony between them, chiefly because Mutti's letters dripped with lament about Vati's parsimony and mental cruelty, whilst Vati's features froze in a hate-filled contort whenever I mentioned my mother during my summer vacations with him in Lindau; he simply could not forgive her for dumping him.

Vati wanted me to live with him in Lindau am Bodensee (at Lake Constance), which would presumably have afforded me a superior education given the outstanding quality of the Bavarian school system. I would also have been spared starvation because my father's wit and ardent oenophilia had quickly won him generous friends among the farmers and vintners in his new neighborhood. But although the

Leipzig divorce court had assigned my mother the sole blame for her failed marriage in 1946, it gave her custody over me, assuming that she was more suitable for this task than my blind father.

Had it been the other way 'round, my childhood would have been less chaotic; then again, my adult life would have turned out less exciting. I might have become a physician, a profession denied to my father due to his war injuries. As it turned out, fate forced me to weave my way around embarrassing grades in mathematics and still achieve success in international journalism, a craft more suitable for my temperament than medicine and arguably more glamorous.

Today, I regret not knowing Vati better, particularly in my adolescence when a boy needs his father most. I fondly remember our wartime walks in Leipzig's woods and our long train ride from Ulm to Hamburg (Chapter 1). I loved the way he told stories. His humor was North German, dry and crisp, much like English wit, whereas mine is typically Saxon; I have been called bouncy and colorful. He liked to come to the point fast; I prefer working many anecdotes into my narrative, delivered in Saxon fashion with the corners of my mouth turned upward. He was no masterly wordsmith when hacking away on the braille-covered keyboard of his portable typewriter, but he was a superb raconteur. We would have complemented each other well if only we had been given a chance to bond.

Throughout my teens, I was an urchin divided, spending my summer breaks with Vati in Bavaria and my Christmas holidays with Mutti and Omi in Communist eastern Germany, crossing the snow-covered Harz mountains guided by the same Wehrmacht veteran who had led my mother and me from East to West back in August

1947. In my Easter and autumn vacations, I was the guest of relatives, such as my godfather, a doctor near the Danish border.

A bizarre travel experience in a miniature chauffeur-driven limousine preceded my reunion with Vati in the summer of 1948. I could hear it from afar as it sputtered, groaned, and flatulated up the steep mountain hill leading from the Ellertal (Eller Valley) to Schloß Hamborn.

Rhooom-boom-boom-boom-boom-boom, it screeched as the driver furiously shifted its three forward gears, trying to overtake the school's horse cart pulled by Lotte and Liese with Wolfgang von Gahlen, the feeble-minded count, at the reins. *Rhooom-boom-boom-boom, boom-boom-boom*, the thing howled, blasting thick blue fumes from its shivering exhaust pipe. I remember thinking, "Oh, my God, here come my wheels. What a joy ride this is going to be!"

The car, licensed by the French military government, was one of the most elegant small vehicles ever built by the German automobile industry before the war: a 1938 front-wheel-drive DKW F-7 Meisterklasse with a top speed of 50 miles per hour! Much about it was marked by the number two. It had a two-stroke engine with two cylinders. It ran on two types of fuel: 40 parts of gasoline mixed with one part of motor oil. It had only two doors and was two-tone. Its roof, long radiator hood, and beautifully curved fenders were black, whilst the rest of its body was Bordeaux-red.

The chauffeur was an awkward-looking lout in white gloves. In a pretentious swerve, he parked his rattling vehicle in front of the castle, jumped out, and opened the passenger's door to an elegantly attired gentleman with the air of a grandee more fitting a luxurious Horch, Mercedes, or Rolls Royce than a blubbering little auto. I had met him in his house in Hamburg: He was Dr. Carl Klügmann, who would have been my grandfather had Mutti not stolen Vati from his fiancée, Natti Klügmann. "Call me Uncle Carl, Uwe," he said, "I am taking you to your father. We shall have much time together."

Uncle Carl ordered his chauffeur to prepare a picnic for himself and me at an enchanting clearing. We pupils had been told it was the favorite place of the poetess Annette von Droste-Hülshoff (1797–1848) when her family owned Schloß Hamborn.

"I so love her poetry! How pleasant to have lunch at a spot where she wrote much of it," said Dr. Klügmann. He began to recite her sonnet "In the Grass," one of her loveliest works, which reads in English:

> Sweet rest, sweet whirls in the grass,
> the fragrant breath of herbs around you,
> a deep, deep, drunken surging,
> as the clouds, like smoke, fade into the blue,
> when round my dizzy drunken head,
> sweet laughter breaks in waves,
> loved voices whisper and drift,
> like lime-blossom onto graves.

> Then, when the dead are in your breast,
> every corpse stirs and stretches,
> softly, softly draws in breath,
> moves the closed eyelashes,
> dead love, dead joy, dead time,
> all these treasures buried, ruined,
> touch themselves with a timid note,
> like tiny bells played by the wind.

Hours, more fleeting than the kiss
a sunbeam gives the morning lake,
than the migrating birds' song,
which, like pearls from the sky, fall on me, flake on flake,
than the iridescent beetle's flash,
as he hurries over his sunny path,
than the hot pressure of a hand,
squeezing its last.

Yet, heaven, give me only this,
I ask you: only for the song,
of every free bird in the blue,
a soul, to bear the song along.
Only for each scanty ray,
my hem of color, sparkling stream,
for every hand that's warm, my grasp,
and for each happiness, a dream.

Uncle Carl stopped, stared at his driver almost with embarrassment, and pointed at a shady spot under a 600-year-old elm tree near Lotte's and Liese's stable on the opposite side of the park.

"Go over there. Refuel the car, have lunch, and sleep for at least one hour. We have a long journey ahead of us," he ordered him.

"Refuel? Where, Uncle Carl?" I asked him. "Are there filling stations anywhere on the roads to Lindau? Gasoline is so scarce around here that the school's Opel Blitz truck runs on gasified wood."

He pointed to the four 20-litre jerricans on his car's roof, saying: "That will easily get us to the nearest military base in the French zone." Now I remembered what Vati had told me about Uncle Carl's lofty position: Having been public trustee of enemy assets in German-occupied Paris, he was now custodian of Nazi properties in the French zone of Germany.

"Why would you not let the chauffeur eat with us?" I asked Uncle Carl when the man had left.

"Because he is a vile character; you'll find out during our trip to Lindau tonight. "God knows where the French have picked him up. I dare not think what he did in the war. Just wait and see!"

"How come you picked me up with your staff car, Uncle Carl?" I asked.

"I am going to reopen my office in our villa in Hamburg and have to take lots of files from our house in Lindau."

Uncle Carl's Hamburg maid had supplied us with plenty of food: Liverwurst sandwiches, blutwurst (blood sausage) sandwiches, pickled cucumbers, hard-boiled eggs, and fruit from Lake Constance, plus some local wine, of which he allowed me half a glass.

Lunch lasted thirty minutes, after which we rested for one hour. Uncle Carl and I were at the poetess' favorite spot, the driver under the old elm tree. Then, off we drove through the glorious eastern Westphalian countryside and past bombed-out towns and industrial cities.

As dusk fell, I was curled up in the back seat with my head resting on my suitcase. I fell asleep. Suddenly, though, I woke in the middle of the night and felt seasick because the small DKW zig-zagged across an autobahn. Looking across the chauffeur's shoulder, I realized what he had in his headlights: hundreds of frogs hopping from one side of the road to another. The driver shrieked with delight as the white amphibians crunched under our wheels.

"Stop this!" Uncle Carl ordered him.

"But, Herr Doktor, surely I am allowed a little fun to keep me awake on this long journey?"

"Fun?" Uncle Carl retorted. "You call killing little critters fun?"

"A few years ago, we were allowed to kill bigger species, Sir!"

"I bet!" said Uncle Carl. "You are monstrous! If you don't stop at once, I will drive Uwe to Lindau, and you can hitchhike. Good luck! I don't see any other vehicles on this road."

The driver drove on, growling but not lurching, and Uncle Carl turned around to me and gave me a meaningful look as if to say, "What did I tell you at Annette von Droste-Hülshoff's corner? We have despicable monsters in this country!"

When we arrived at the Klügmann's elegant summer home in Lindau, he ordered the chauffeur to park the DKW in his garage and, turning to the house, told me, "You'll never see this despicable man again because this afternoon, I am going to ask the French to investigate his past."

The last thing I heard of him was that he was serving a long prison sentence for Nazi crimes, which made me think, "Strange how the French military government employed a former SS man. What a goofy bunch of conquerors!"

Vati smiled from ear to ear as he hugged me. He told me to sleep in his room.

"And you?"

"I'll spend the night in the bed of the lady who couldn't cut my meat because of her lame arm. Remember that story?"

"I do, but is she not married to Paul Schmidt, Uncle Carl's right-hand man?"

"He is Uncle Carl's right-hand man, but he is now another woman's lover."

"Hmmm!"

"Sleep well, *mein Junge* (my boy)!"

When I awoke a few hours later, I noticed someone fumbling with my mouth. It was Vati trying to slip a piece of chocolate between my lips, the sweetest gesture I remember of our relationship, which turned more and more bitter with every summer vacation I spent at his ground-floor apartment in the lakeside villa he moved into after breaking up with the lame Klügmann daughter.

The villa belonged to a Bavarian countess with a fondness for this blind, forever sun-tanned Herr Doktor war hero, who in turn preferred the company of delicious seniors from a girls' school provided to him by its lesbian deputy principal. Supposedly, they kept him company as his "readers." It didn't take me long to discover that Vati's interest in them went beyond literature.

Once, when I was about 15 or 16, I picked him up by train from a cure in a home for the war-blind in the Black Forest.

"I have a new reader," Vati informed me. "Her name is Theresa."

"Is she pretty?"

"Not really," he answered, "You know I prefer slender women. Theresa is more of the comely type."

When we arrived at Lindau *Hauptbahnhof* (central station), Theresa was there. She was comely indeed! In fact, she was magnificent! If Vati didn't find her attractive (how, by the way, did he, as a blind man, discern her figure?), I most certainly did! We took a taxi to Vati's apartment, where the countess had already prepared supper for us.

"Take Theresa home," my father commanded, "Use my tandem," meaning the two-seater bicycle that the *Versorgungsamt*, as the German VA is called, had provided for blind war veterans. We biked past haystacks, found one of them alluring, and decided to repeat our activity there on my father's couch the next morning while he swam to a rock in Lake Constance; Vati managed to get there and back following the sunlight, which his one eye, though blind, could make out.

One morning, he didn't swim, however. Instead, though clad in swimming trunks, he hid in a hall closet. While Theresa and I were making merry on the sofa, I suddenly felt an excruciating pain on my rear. I turned around and saw my father, naked except for his trunks, angrily clobbering my rear with his ivory-topped cane (which I still possess). That same afternoon, he bundled me off to Hagen in Westphalia, where my mother lived.

Despite all that, he invited me back to Lindau the next summer. He picked me up at the *Hauptbahnhof*, this time accompanied by two "readers": Theresa on his right and a marginally less attractive girl on his left. "This one," he said, pointing to the less attractive girl, "is yours." "But that one," Vati continued, grabbing Theresa's gloriously plump upper arm, "You will have to leave to me." We spent six wonderful weeks together.

I admit that my father's morals had limitations, as had my mother's. Their relationship reached its bitterest moment when they had to share a room at my confirmation at Schloß Hamborn in April 1951. He had come from Lindau; she had fled from East Germany. They could not hide their hatred for one another, which I deeply resented. Now, I resent myself for this resentment. Like so many children of divorced parents, I quite irrationally felt guilty for the breakup of Vati's and Mutti's marriage. I don't anymore because I realize that this was nuts.

Late in life, I regret not having nurtured my bond with my father and not having found out more about his life before he was blinded, how he was blinded, how he managed to graduate from high school and the law school at Leipzig University, and how he managed to earn his "doctorate of both laws" (secular and ecclesiastical).

Mutti made light of these accomplishments; I fault myself for not having applied to my father the stringent curiosity that should be the mark of every good journalist.

The author with his mother, Ruth, and his father, Karl-Heinz, at his confirmation in his boarding school Schloß Hamburg in April 1951. His parents hated each other.

CHAPTER 6

Breaking Points in Urchin's Life

TWO BREAKING POINTS MARKED my life as an urban urchin at a rural boarding school. The first was the *Währungsreform*, the currency reform in the three western zones of Germany that soon triggered the Wirtschaftswunder, or "economic miracle."[1] The second was my confirmation three years later, which was the beginning of the end of my stay in Schloß Hamborn. I shall get to that presently.

At Sunday breakfast on June 20, 1948, Herr Pickert, our headmaster, banged a spoon against his coffee cup and announced:

"Children, today is our last day of hunger. This morning, a new hard currency was introduced. It is called the Deutsche Mark (German Mark). Tomorrow, the shops will be full of things we haven't seen since the beginning of the war."

---

1 On June 20, 1948, the Deutsche Mark (DM) was introduced as the only valid new currency in the three western occupation zones of Germany. The old Reichsmark was worth nothing from that day on. For this new beginning, every citizen received a per capita allowance of DM 40, and a further allowance of DM 20 one month later. Savings balances were revalued at a ratio of 10:1—for 100 Reichsmarks, 10 DM were credited. Large assets were ex-changed at the rate of 0.65 DM (65 pfennigs) per 10 Reichsmarks.

At once, we children stopped moaning about the meager meal before us and were excitedly looking forward to Monday. We had already known since Saturday that something big was going to happen.

"Let's go to Paderborn, children," suggested Fräulein Rassmann, our class teacher, after morning prayers.

"Why, Fräulein Rassmann?" we moaned. "This is our day off!"

"If we visit Paderborn today and then again on Monday, you will witness a historic transformation of our country. Trust me!"

We trusted her and went.

The road to Paderborn looked as depressing as it had at my arrival half a year earlier. It was covered with potholes, and the roadside was littered with debris from the last days of combat: burned-out German and American tanks, trucks, and jeeps. The vehicles passing us were either horse carts or cars and lorries propelled by wood gasifiers, for gasoline was rare. Fräulein Rassmann pointed to a spot close to Schloß Hamborn where Maj. Gen. Maurice Rose, commander of the 3rd U.S. Armored Division, had lost his life in fierce combat with the SS Brigade Westfalen a little more than three years earlier.

However, we saw the first signs of an impending recovery in the city. All the streets had been cleared of rubble, the trams were running as scheduled, and more and more residents had moved back into their ravaged homes, turning their basements and ground floors into temporary dwellings. The black market behind the cathedral, usually a lively place on Saturdays, seemed almost dead; many regular stores were closed to allow their owners to stock their shelves with treasures for sale the following week.

On Monday morning, our headmaster told us pupils to line up at their class teachers' desks to receive 40 DM each, as prescribed by the currency reform law for every West German, children included.

"Let's go shopping," said Fräulein Rassmann and guided us back to Paderborn, which had been transformed overnight. Delights many of us had never known, such as bananas, oranges, coconuts, and pineapples, filled shop windows. The shelves were laden with bags of first-class coffee beans, chocolates, pralines, marzipan, and other delicacies. I bought one kilo (2.2 lbs.) of raisins for DM 1.80 and told Fräulein Rassmann I would take them to Omi and Mutti in Leipzig as a Christmas present.[2]

I came to rue this decision five months later as I crossed illegally from the British to the Soviet zones during my Christmas break. Mutti had organized for me to meet a border guide in the western foothills of the Harz mountains. The guide had seven clients for the crossing; I was the only child among them; the other six were adults, including a hysterical woman whose shrieks almost caused us to get shot.

We set off on a steep, six-hour uphill hike at 11:00 p.m. The kilo of raisins in my rucksack weighed heavily on my back as I trudged through thick snow and as more fell relentlessly. Our guide carefully steered us through a forest, but it thinned as we climbed higher and higher. We arrived at a clearing and heard male voices from the eastern side of the demarcation line. A flashlight shone in our direction. "Communist border guards," whispered our guide. The woman

---

2 In eastern Germany, the Soviet occupation introduced a different new currency, also called the Mark. But it was worth little, and compared with shops in the western zone, the eastern German stores were quite barren. Bananas, oranges, and the like remained rare until the Communist regime collapsed in November 1989.

screamed. The guide grabbed her by the scruff of her neck and shoved her face first, deep into the snow. "Shhh! Down!" he ordered us. We obeyed.

We sank into the snow and, therefore, out of sight of Soviet or East German border guards. They were close, and I feared that they might have discovered us. But they hadn't. Our guide made us retreat about 100 yards back to the western side. I could still see their flashlights; still, they missed us. We crawled further into the forest and waited until the border guards left. Then we got up and walked to the peak where we crossed the frontier. Drenched in sweat, we descended to a village where the guide dropped me off at a tiny railway station.

Mutti was already there with third-class train tickets for both of us and a Montblanc pen as a reward for the guide. I decided to give her the raisins, thankful I hadn't thrown them away on my long mountain march. She looked haggard, skinny, and undernourished. When we arrived in Leipzig, I asked Omi,

"What's the matter with Mutti?"

"She is very ill," she answered. "She is suffering from cartilage dissolution and needs urgent treatment but can't get it here. Go and see your Uncle Carl; perhaps he can help."

I took the number 24 tram to Springerstraße 21, home of Dr. Carl Ballin, my father's fraternity brother who had been my favorite companion during the war. He was a chemist, but as the former owner and director of the Leipzig Inhalatorium und Radium Emanatorium, a nationally renowned institution treating respiratory diseases, he was also an accomplished diagnostician.

"Can you please help Mutti?" I asked him, adding, "Although, Uncle Carl, you actually look just as awful as she."

BREAKING POINTS IN URCHIN'S LIFE

"That's how one looks after five months in a Communist prison," he answered. "They nearly starved me to death. But I am on the mend."

"What were you in jail for, Uncle Carl?"

"I had smuggled medicines from West Berlin to the Soviet zone to treat very ill patients of mine. The People's Police caught me on the train home. I was sentenced to five years and the expropriation of my Inhalatorium. Then they realized that they had nobody else to run it. So, they let me go and reinstated me as its director, though not as owner."

"I am very concerned about Mutti."

"I know. She has already come to see me. She was in a frightening state. She has been starving since losing her position at the Sächsische Landesbank, where she organized cultural events for the bank's staff and customers. Didn't you know this?"

"No. Why was she fired?"

"If your Mutti's condition weren't so dangerous, this would be a funny story," Uncle Carl went on. "The FDGB[3] chapter at the bank commissioned her to draft, for its annual concert, a program of music from many countries. But the program had to first pass muster by a Soviet commissar. He loved it because it featured a piece called *Rhapsodie in Blau* by a certain Russian named Georgy Gershwynov."

"Georgy Gershwynov? I have never heard of him," I interjected.

"Nobody has; that's just the point," said Uncle Carl, laughing. "A Red Army colonel with some knowledge of Western music sat in the

---

3 FDGB stood for the Communist *Freier Deutscher Gewerkschaftsbund*, or Free German Trade Union Federation. Founded in 1946, it was the only union allowed to operate in the Soviet zone, which then became the German Democratic Republic (East Germany).

• 73 •

audience. When the applause died down, he turned to the commissar, saying. 'He-he-he Товарищ (comrade), 'you have been taken for a ride. There is no Russian composer called Georgy Gershwynov. We just heard *Rhapsody in Blue* by George Gershwin, an American—a class enemy! You, comrade, have allowed this woman to sneak in a class enemy, he-he-he!'"

"Were you there, Uncle Carl?"

"No, but I heard about her caper while behind bars. Bless your mother! Her lark cheered me at a time I needed it most. I never thought she had such a wicked sense of irony."

"Sometimes she does, not often. Humor is my father's strong point. What happened then?"

"She was dismissed and put on the lowest possible ration of 700 calories a day."

"What can be done about her health?"

"She needs massive doses of nutrients, such as vitamins, calories, lipids, and proteins. Cod liver oil would be the most effective remedy, but you can't get it here. I am looking for some brave soul willing to travel to West Berlin and bring back plenty of that stuff."[4]

"God, I should have brought Mutti fish oil instead of raisins!"

"You didn't know, Uwe, and at any rate, you couldn't have carried more than one bottle. Lots of bottles are needed in her case."

I did not see Mutti again until my confirmation more than two years later. Mutti wrote that her condition was worsening, although visitors to West Berlin occasionally bought her the fish oil. I tried to send her a bottle per month; sometimes, it arrived in Leipzig,

---

4 Back in 1948, East Germans were still allowed to travel to West Berlin. The Berlin Wall was not built until 1961.

but more often, it did not. I began running out of my hard, new D-Marks.

I spent my summer holidays with my father in Lindau on the shore of Lake Constance. By now, he lived well on his civil service pension and war disability allowance.

"Please, Vati, help me pay for Mutti's cod liver oil," I implored him.

Vati's face hardened. "She left me. She left you. Why should I now buy her cod liver oil? For that matter, why are you doing this?"

"She is my mother, and I love her and don't want her to die."

"Do what you must, but don't count on me. If you want a better life, why not move down here to Bavaria and live with me?"

"Mutti would not agree. Switching from the Rudolf Steiner school system to a Bavarian gymnasium at this stage would be nearly impossible. Moreover, being blind, you would not be able to supervise my homework!"

"A friend of mine is the deputy principal of the girl's high school here in Lindau; she is quite willing to check your work and would do a better job of it than your tutors at Schloß Hamborn."

"That's true. Is this lady your girlfriend, Vati?"

"No. She is older than I and will soon retire. Moreover, she prefers women."

"EEEEE! What does she do for you?"

"She sends me seniors from her school as readers."

"Let's talk about my future with Mutti when the three of us meet at my confirmation," I suggested.

(No answer).

I was confirmed in April 1951 in the Weiße Saal (White Hall) of Schloß Hamborn. The officiant was the *Lenker*, the Hamburg-based "bishop" (of sorts) of the Christian Community, an esoteric church linked to anthroposophy. The Christian Community claimed to have "no doctrine"; each priest could preach whatever he pleased. Nonetheless, in my preparation classes, I was taught reincarnation. When my physical body disappears, I learned, my "astral body" would be sent to a space called Karmaloca to suffer for all the bad things I had done on earth; only then would I receive a new body of flesh and blood.

My confirmation was a bizarre happening—liturgically whacky and, for me, personally unpleasant. I was squeezed in between my parents, both exquisitely ill-tempered because they were forced upon each other by a shortage of rooms: a hate-filled divorced couple compelled to share a small chamber. Vati was furious, especially as in teetotaling Schloß Hamborn, there was not even wine to render him merry.

Mutti had arrived from Leipzig with both legs in casts, hence almost lame. The East German authorities had issued her an exit permit, expecting her not to return. As she said matter-of-factly: "It would have become too expensive for the Communists to keep me alive." Her attempt to cuddle up with her ex-husband proved futile. "Stay away from me, woman!" he snarled, according to her.

The Christian Community's worship service is called "Act of Consecration of Man"; to Vati, it was so bizarre that his facial expression vacillated from dour (when he smelled incense, to which he was allergic) to sardonic when listening to the turgid liturgy of this arcane sect. Once, though, he laughed out loud, as did many other parents. This happened when he was told that I had perpetrated a scandalous booboo when receiving Communion. In my younger years, I had been told that Confirmation was the moment when young Lutherans are allowed alcohol for the first time. My happy anticipation was dismally disappointed.

In the Service of the Sacrament, the *Lenker* handed me the common cup. Greedily, I took a big gulp. But instead of the wine I had expected, a revoltingly sweet grape juice filled the caverns of my mouth, making me cough and splutter quite violently. A huge gob of spittle emanating from my mouth colored much of the cleric's Alb red. The *Lenker* stopped the service momentarily to stare dolefully at his soiled vestment. Half the congregation found this scene mirthful; anthroposophical hardliners were outraged.

"*Aus Dir wird nie etwas werden*" (nothing will ever become of you), hissed *Gräfin* (countess) K., Schloß Hamborn's head tutor for girls, as I left the Weiße Saal after the service; she could never hide her distaste for me, the loud-mouthed prankster from Leipzig.

Had the *Gräfin* been able to look into my head, her loathing of me would have increased manifold, for as I was leaving the incense-filled Weiße Saal, I vowed that I would return to the Lutheran faith my Omi had taught me in her Leipzig air raid shelter. My strange confirmation rite had made me realize that I must side with Luther's doctrine, promising salvation by grace alone and through faith in Christ alone, rather than going through the rest of my life fearing that my "astral body" would be dumped in Karmaloca. I stared coldly at the countess, dreading that she might be in charge of my suffering in that grisly space for my sins on earth.

Heading toward the dining room for my confirmation luncheon, the thought occurred to me that, as my departure from Schloß Hamborn was imminent, time was running out for me to pull one last practical joke to annoy the *Gräfin* and others, notably her young lover, a stern former Wehrmacht lieutenant now supervising the boys' dorms on our floor. The opportunity for one last coup arose quite unexpectedly. The residents of the Catholic retirement home run by Vincentine nuns were being moved from the Schloß back to Paderborn, where their building, which had been bombed out in the last days of the war, was being rebuilt.

As these seniors and the sisters freed Schloß Hamborn room by room and floor by floor, *Gräfin* K's lover, the former Wehrmacht lieutenant, delegated us boys to move furniture to the castle's attic, whence we had easy access to the movement of the massive tower clock, the bells of which thundered every hour on the hour to call on us children to get out of bed, go to prayers, the dining room, and class.

I called a confab of boys who, like me, had always wondered whether nuns were bald.

"Here is perhaps our last chance to find out," I said.

"How?"

"Have you noticed that the sisters retire to their rooms after lunch every day and then come out when the tower clock rings at 3:00 p.m.?"

"Y-e-e-e-s?"

"We must assume that they remove their hoods before their siesta, mustn't we?"

"Y-e-e-e-s?"

"So, here's my plan: When they are in bed, snoozing for an hour, we set the tower clock to 3:00 p.m., and then, boing, boing, boing, the bell will shake them awake. Like headless chickens, they will come rushing out of their rooms. We can observe them from above, from the attic door. I bet some nuns will be so flustered that they forget to wear their hoods. Then we will find out if they have hair on their heads."

"Let's do it!" the others said, slapping their thighs.

The next day, we realized our plan. We discovered that the nuns' scalps were neither bald nor covered with luscious locks of hair; instead, they resembled the unshaven chins of scruffy old men.

I felt victorious, but not for long. The untimely ring of the tower bell also alarmed the *Gräfin's* paramour. Determined to maintain the school's peaceful coexistence with the departing sisters in their last weeks at Schloß Hamborn, he endeavored to set the clock back, going about it in a manifestly asinine way, though. Instead of moving the hands of the clock forward until he reached the right hour again, say 2:35 p.m., he yanked them backward, an unwise thing to do given that this inevitably screwed up the mechanics of an ancient clock. Hence it got stuck at just after 3:00 p.m., and the bells continued to boom nonstop. A repairman was called.

"There is nothing I can do," said the repairman. "The clockwork must run its course until it is wound down."

"But this can take days. How can we teach or sleep with this racket from the tower?" the ex-lieutenant moaned, giving me a filthy look, prompting me to stare at him with equal hostility. "Who was it that screwed up this system, you or I?" I thought.

I was sentenced to stand behind my chair at every breakfast, lunch, and dinner until the summer break. Seeing her hatred of me vindicated, *Gräfin* K. persuaded the headmaster to inflict an additional punishment on me: I was to remain at Schloß Hamborn one more week after all my schoolmates had gone home.

I was quite happy about this decision: I had the dorm to myself; there were no classes to attend; I could enjoy the beautiful country- side around the school, knowing that I would not be back after the summer because by then, I would be living with Mutti in the gritty industrial city of Hagen.

The losers were the vengeful countess and her fellow esotericists. Now, they had to endure and feed me even longer and watch that I did not pull another prank on them as a parting shot. All this defied logic, but logic is not the esotericists' strong point.

CHAPTER 7

Urchin's Dark Years

THE DAY I ARRIVED in Hagen, I asked God in my prayers, "Why did you dump me in this hideous place?" The prospect of spending the rest of my adolescence penniless in this bombed-out industrial city in Westphalia struck me as an undeserved punishment. As it turned out, my stint in Hagen evolved into a thrilling career as a journalist and a wonderful personal life.

So now, I remember Hagen fondly. I particularly cherish the memory of Johannes Kruse, the Lutheran pastor of Emst-Bissingheim and Haßley, a Hagen suburb. He examined me before admitting me to the Lord's Supper. I remember him asking me, for instance:

"What is the highest service a Christian can render to God?"

"To serve my neighbor lovingly in all our earthly endeavors."

"*Donnerwetter* (Wow)!" he exclaimed, "who taught you that?"

"My grandmother in her air raid shelter as bombs dropped on Leipzig."

"And how does one serve one's neighbors under bombs?"

"By not showing fear, my grandmother told me that showing fear is ungentlemanly and un-Christian."

"And how is fearlessness a loving service to the other people in the shelter?"

"It gave them comfort. They saw and heard Omi and me smile and jest and sing hymns. They smiled with us."

"I wish your Omi had been my theology professor at university."

I also think fondly of Hagen's Karl-Ernst Osthaus Museum and its magnificent collection and exhibits of modern art, chiefly paintings. I gratefully recall Herr Beckmann, the cultural editor of *Westfalenpost*, a large regional paper, who launched me into my profession as a reporter based on my knowledge of contemporary paintings.

We met when I brazenly entered his office and walked right up to his desk in the fall of 1952 if I remember correctly.

"Who are you?" he asked.

"Uwe Siemon-Netto, high school pupil."

"And what can I do for you?"

"I am dissatisfied with your cultural pages."

"Well, I am already delighted that a kid your age reads our cultural section," he said with a grin. "How do you think it could be improved?"

"Cover the Karl Ernst Osthaus Museum, the cultural jewel of this town; I spend all my spare time there but hardly ever read anything about it in the *Westfalenpost*."

"Give me an example of what we have failed to cover lately."

"A breathtaking exhibition of the works of Amedeo Modigliani that opened a few days ago."

"Frankly," Herr Beckmann replied with a sad smile, "nobody on my staff understands modern art."

He handed me a few sheets of paper and a pen and said, "Write!"

I penciled a few paragraphs about Modigliani (1884–1920), who was—and still is—one of my favorite painters, and handed the manuscript to him. This established a friendship between us, which eventually paved the way for my career as a journalist.

I'll get to this significant event in my young life later in this volume. But first I must tell my readers how I ended up in Hagen in the first place. Mutti moved there because her friend Inge, the wife of one of my father's fraternity brothers, had fled there immediately after the Soviet occupation of Leipzig. Her husband, Herbert, was an attorney. Whether he had died or divorced her, I can't recall. At any rate, Inge took my mother in and nursed her back to health but also confessed to Mutti that she had been my father's mistress, that Vati had made her pregnant three times, and insisted that my three siblings growing in her womb be aborted. Mutti told me all of this breathlessly when she picked me up at Hagen's central railway station in late August of 1951. It was just the kind of news a teenager loves to hear from and about his parents.

Mutti looked much better than at my confirmation. The casts had been removed from her legs. She seemed well-fed. She took me by tram to her sunny rented room in the outlying district of Emst. She had the use of a well-tended garden where I was allowed to keep my first-ever pet, a 40-year-old tortoise named Eulalia. A friendly dentist drilled a hole into her shell, allowing me to attach her with a long cable to a cherry tree. The animal kept crawling 'round and 'round the tree until her butt scraped its bark. Then she waited patiently for hours until I came to liberate her, whereupon she stuck out her scrawny neck as far as possible in order to kiss me.

"Where am I going to sleep?" I asked Mutti.

"Not here," she said. "I have rented a nice little attic flat for you for only DM 20 a month, and just a 20-minute walk from here. We'll go there after dinner. I hope you can carry your suitcase because I can't afford a taxi."

The suitcase was heavy, and there was nothing nice about my 20-DM flat. Its rooms were minuscule. It had neither a toilet, nor a shower, nor even running water and a washbasin. There was no central heating, just one coke-fired round-iron stove.

"Where do I get the coke from? Where do I dump the ashes?" I asked the landlady.

"You will have to figure that out by yourself," she replied coolly. "In our part of the house, we have central heating; that's all I know."

"And where do I relieve myself? Where do I shower?"

"You may use our bathroom, but not before 8:00 a.m."

"By that time, I am in school."

"That's not my problem," the landlady answered.

Turning to my mother, I said, "This won't work."

"Never mind," she said, "You can always come to me, do your business, and keep warm."

These were grisly prospects. Mutti had enrolled me at the Waldorf School in Wuppertal-Unterbarmen, a 40-minute journey on a steam train from Hagen Central. To get to the station from Emst involved a 20-minute streetcar ride, which in turn required a 15-minute walk from my attic flat. Altogether, the fastest I could make it from home to school was 75 minutes, usually more.

To save time and the 40-pfennig round trip tram fare, I decided to walk to the depot, which was easy downhill in the morning but more cumbersome in the evening. The latter had the sizzling advantage that my route went right through the red-light street, where I often stopped to ogle. Once, I even asked a comely black-haired prostitute if she would be so kind as to teach me the art of making love. She looked up and down the street and asked me, "How old are you?"

"Sixteen."

"Far too young, but you are cute. Come through the back door and make sure a policeman does not see you."

At the back door, she asked me: "How much money do you have?"

"Five marks."

"Five marks? I am not running a charity."

"It's all I have, and you said I was cute."

She laughed: "You are. Come in. When you leave, you won't be a virgin anymore, and then you'll be on your own."

It was already dark when I left the bordello. I didn't bother to stop at my mother's home but went to a sausage stand instead, had a *bratwurst*, and elatedly walked to my attic flat. On my way to that grim place, I decided I didn't want to be lonely anymore. I picked up a hedgehog crawling across the street. It evidently felt comfortable in my warm hand.

Next to my bed was an opening leading to a dark space under the roof, which I assigned to my hedgehog and two others I caught in the following days. In true pig fashion, they separated their new dwelling into a living space closest to my bed and a toilet section further back where it could not be seen, but it stank. Soon, my apartment smelled like a pig pen. I decided to live with this until the spring when I released the animals into nature.

When I returned home from school, they greeted me lovingly, knowing they would be allowed to share the sandwiches my mother had prepared for my morning break at school. Quenching their thirst was problematic in the winter. There was a bucket of water in my living room, but it had turned quickly into a giant block of ice. So, I went downstairs with a pot and filled it with snow, which I melted with an immersion heater. My smart hedgehogs drank it rapidly, probably knowing the melted snow would soon turn into ice.

The hedgehogs were being taken care of, so I took off my clothes, wrapped myself quickly in my bathrobe, went to bed, and resolved to end this charade of my life quickly. I stopped begging my landlady to let me use her bathroom but urinated instead out of my skylight onto the roof when the need arose at night; I relieved myself more thoroughly and then washed in the morning on the train to Wuppertal. If there was time left, I devoted it to doing my homework in my compartment while eating a Frankfurter I had bought from a sausage man on the platform at the Hagen railway station for 1 DM apiece.

For that, I needed money. Hence, I determined to make myself financially more independent from my mother, who received DM 150 per month from Vati to keep me but didn't try very hard to find an adequate job for herself in the height of the German Wirtschaftswunder when highly educated and multi-lingual young women like Mutti were urgently sought after. She sang for 20 DM at weddings and funerals and occasionally for a little more at a cantata service in church.

She was offered a position as a mezzo-soprano in the professional choir of West German Radio (WDR) in Cologne. This way, she would have been a civil servant with a good pension at the end of her career. But she rejected this proposition brusquely, saying, "I am a soloist, not a chorister."

When she told me this, I resolved to seek alternative sources of food and income. The former I found at the Hotel zur Post in Wuppertal-Elberfeld, where my parents and I had stayed during the war when visiting Klaus G., a prominent textile industrialist we knew from our winter holidays in Schloß Elmau in Bavaria. Now a penurious divorcee in nearby Hagen, Mutti figured that she, still young and fetching, might become this permanent bachelor's wife, even if his libidinous inclinations drew him in an entirely different direction.

"Never mind, every important man, including one of those, needs a strong and beautiful woman on his side," she said. Klaus G. visited her in Hagen. They walked in the woods where Mutti tried to seduce him, only to trigger a reaction similar to that she received from the Prince-Heir of the Grand-Duchy of Saxony-Altenburg when she had propositioned him in Schloß Hamborn. "*Ach, gnädige Frau* (gracious lady), I am just too degenerate for that sort of thing." So back she was in her rented room in Hagen-Emst, neither a princess nor an industrialist's wife.

Still, Klaus G. rendered me a kind service. He talked to his friend, the owner of the Hotel zur Post, on my behalf and persuaded him to feed me a plate of potatoes and gravy with occasionally a scrap of meat or a few peas or carrots thrown in for one DM every weekday. My hunger sated, I walked into the office of the HR manager of Kaufhof, the Elberfeld branch of a chain of department stores. He led me to the food and drinks department and said,

"We urgently need sales interns here. What would you like to sell?"

"Wine," I said.

"O.K., you can start now."

I was in hog heaven, advising customers on what tipple they should buy, having diligently studied all the bumph on the back labels of the wine bottles.

The customers were bemused by this kid flogging wine and bought so much that after a few weeks, my success came to the attention of the general manager, who dropped by to see me.

"How old are you, *um Gottes Willen* (for God's sake)?" he asked me.

"Sixteen."

"Sixteen? It is against the law for anyone under the age of twenty-one to sell alcohol!"

"But, Sir, I am selling a lot of your wine."

"Never you mind. Do you, little fool, believe I am willing to go to jail for allowing you to sell wine? No, my boy, I am going to transfer you to an office, period!"

Sorrowfully, I left my wine racks and moved into the head book-keeper's office. The two of us were ill-matched. He was an appalling philistine with a special loathing for this loud-mouthed little Saxon working at the desk in front of his. I resented being bullied by this little man, and so, one day, after having a bowl of pea soup for lunch at the Hotel zur Post in lieu of my usual spuds with gravy, I had had enough of his verbal chicanery. Given that he sat immediately behind me, I flatulated massively into his face. He rang HR, and ten minutes later, I was out on the street, but not for long.

I walked into the front office of a nearby small textile mill and asked to be shown to the boss. I realized this showed some chutzpah, but surprisingly, it worked. I was taken to the office of a beautiful woman, the widow of an industrialist who had died in the war. She was petite, perhaps 35 years old, dark-haired, with a gorgeous figure and smiling eyes.

"What can I do for you?" she asked, clearly bemused by my visit.

"I need a job, *gnädige Frau* (gracious lady)."

"What can you do for me?"

"Carry bales of textiles."

"You are hired."

I was happy. I earned more money than in the department store and saw this lovely lady daily. Once, she asked me, "Uwe, why did Kaufhof fire you?"

"I farted into the head bookkeeper's face," I answered, whereupon she laughed and laughed until tears dropped from her glorious brown eyes.

"This is the funniest reason for a dismissal I have ever heard," she said, embracing me warmly. I had her beautiful scent in my nose for many days and remember this episode to this day as the most erotic experience of my adolescence.

My platonic romance with my boss was short-lived because my dismal performance at the Waldorf School forced my parents to a rare understanding. They agreed that I wasn't worth the tuition for private education, plus the train fare. So, Mutti enrolled me, free of charge, at the municipal Fichte-Gymnasium in Hagen, where I didn't do any better.

I was an A student in German, English, art, music, religion, and history, but an utter failure in mathematics and physics. When my class was given a quiz, I caricatured the teacher instead of solving the assigned problem and handed in my drawing at the end of class (see image). The teacher didn't know whether he should laugh or be rightfully angry when he recognized himself in my depiction of him. German schools grade from 1 (very good) to 6 (extremely bad). So, he wrote into the class book, "Grinding my teeth, I give Uwe a 6 because this is the worst grade allowed in the state of North Rhine Westphalia; he deserves a 7."

In 12th grade, one year before the *Abitur*, the German high school final examination qualifying students for university studies, the principal asked my mother and me to his office.

Caricature of the author's mathematics teacher
in Hagen. The author drew it instead of solving a
quiz in class.

"Uwe," he said, "We don't know what to do with you. All your
teachers are at a loss. Your report card reads like the Alps, all high
peaks and deep ravines. You are best in class in German; you are a
wonderful writer. You are very artistic, know more about music and
religion than all the others, and do very well in English. But with a 6
in mathematics, you'll never make it to university. What do you want
to do with your life when you leave school?"

"I would either like to become a caricaturist/painter," I said, making the principal snigger.

"Your caricatural talent has not escaped our faculty's attention,"
he said, "but what else?"

"A journalist."

"We thought so and have made inquiries," he answered. "There is a renowned journalism school in Aachen, but it requires that its students have the Abitur." He didn't know that in those days, most German journalists were trained not academically but in a rigorous two-year internship called *Volontariat*.

"And what if I wanted to become an artist?"

"Well, that looks better. Your art teacher has taken the liberty of sending some of your drawings and watercolors to the Akademie der Bildenden Künste (art school) in Munich. They were quite impressed and suggested you come down, meet members of the faculty, and sit an exam."

I liked this idea, but my blind father did not. "I am not going to fund the art studies of a bum who'll never earn a living," he wrote. "But perhaps you can opt for applied arts and get a real job." I discussed this with my art teacher at school. "Your father is right," he said, "and I know the perfect man for you to study with in Munich. His name is Professor Anton Marxmüller. Show him your caricatures. I bet he loves them as much as I do."

Having dropped out of the Fichte-Gymnasium, I hitchhiked from Hagen to Munich in the fall of 1954 to meet Professor Marxmüller. In my rucksack, I carried my latest drawings, watercolors, and tempera paintings. Marxmüller told me that he enjoyed my work very much but could not take me on as a student immediately. "Firstly, you'll have to pass an entrance examination, which I am sure you'll pass," he said, "but secondly, I'll be on sabbatical all next year. Come back to see me in 1956."

"I'll do that," I answered before hitchhiking home to Hagen, catching a fierce cold this time on the back seat of a BMW motorbike. But I never returned to Professor Marxmüller, for, in 1955, my life took an entirely different turn. I decided that before starting an artistic career, I must improve my English and French. First, I wanted to work in Great Britain, regardless of what job I was offered. It turned out that the National Farmers' Union had converted former POW camps with Nissen huts[1] into dwellings for young foreigners willing to harvest fruit, shift manure, lift bales of hay to lorries, build dams, feed chickens, drive tractors, and pick potatoes. This was the easiest way to obtain a work permit and a visa.

I applied, but the bureaucratic process was egregiously slow. Mutti and I had now moved into much pleasanter rooms in the elegant villa of the owner of a drop forge manufacturing axles and car joints for Volkswagen and Borgward.

"Why don't you work in my factory while waiting for your British visa?" he suggested.

"Wonderful. But what can I do for you?"

"You could drive electric carts or work in my quality control department."

This seemed more fun than school, but then I drove a cart laden with Borgward axles onto a scale, neglecting to secure the vehicle properly. Suddenly, the monstrous machine moved forward and rolled over my right foot, breaking all five toes. I spent six weeks in hospital, though with full pay, which proved handy later in the UK. My discharge from the hospital coincided with the arrival of my British visa. Still limping, I hitchhiked to the port of Ostend in Belgium, whence I took a ferry to Folkestone in Kent.

---

1 A Nissen hut is a prefabricated steel structure originally for military use, especially as barracks, made from a half-cylindrical skin of corrugated iron. The Nissen Hut was smaller than American Quonset Huts, and it employed two layers of corrugated steel sheets on the lower sides and a single sheet above the roof.

CHAPTER 8

Urchin's English Liaisons

"IT TOOK ME A long time to figure you out, Uwe," admitted Hans-Albrecht Schraepler, the erstwhile press attaché at the West German embassy in Saigon, when he telephoned me shortly before his death a few years ago. He went on, "Eventually, it dawned on me: This guy is an adventurer."

Come to think of it, he was right. I was an adventurer in the sense that I was a curious reporter. My curiosity and some of its consequences will be the subject of this chapter. It will include tales of my first romantic experiences. Nothing pornographic will tarnish these pages. But I cannot leave out these extraordinary adventures, for they were a memorable part of my transition from puberty to adulthood, a transition that occurred in England.

I became abundantly aware of the extent of my thirst for knowledge in late April 1955 when the ferry from Belgium docked in Folkestone. I rejoiced about overcoming my unpleasant early teenage years, including my abject failure at school and my loveless life in an attic flat without water and heat. My relief must have shown on my face. I smiled.

"You seem a happy young man. Where are you going?" asked the elegantly dressed driver of a superb green 1.5-liter Riley limousine immediately after I had left the ship, passed Immigration, and set out to hitchhike north.

"To London and then Yorkshire," I said.

"Where in London?"

"A youth hostel."

"We can take you as far as London."

In the youth hostel, I met a dozen German speakers. None admitted to being a German because they were ashamed of their national identity. Some posed as Luxembourgers, others as Swiss, Dutch, and even Austrians, which I found particularly stupid given that they identified with a country that had spawned Hitler.

"Why do you have a German flag on your rucksack?" asked a man in his late twenties, old enough to have served in the Wehrmacht. He

In 1955, the author spent almost one year in England. Just off the ferry, he was given a lift in a green Riley, the most beautiful British car at that time.

had just arrived in England by freighter from Pakistan, where he taught German. "The English will never give you a lift when they see that. They hate us."

"When I came up from Folkestone, that flag didn't stop people from giving me a lift," I retorted. "Quite to the contrary."

"Oomph," replied the senior lecturer from Peshawar.

The next morning, I stood thumbing at a roundabout in Mill Hill in northern London, the perfect starting point for hitchhikers heading upwards on the A-1, also known as the Great North Road. What happened then was so beautiful that I have kept every facet of it in my heart until this very day. I waited less than two minutes when a pre-war Bentley stopped. Its sides were ivory-colored, its top, bonnet, and fenders black.

"*Wohin möchten Sie* (where would you like to go)?" asked the driver, a gentleman perhaps in his late forties, in German.

"*Nach York, bitte* (to York, please)," I said.

"*Bitte steigen Sie ein* (please get in), I am going to Leeds. We will spend many hours together on this road until I must turn West, and you will have to go East. I liked the German tricolor on your rucksack and thought this might be a chance to brush up on my German again; I have not spoken the language of Goethe since before the war. You, in turn, are presumably here to improve your English. So, let's do this: I address you in German and you correct me, and you speak to me in English, and I'll correct you, *einverstanden* (alright)?"

"*Einverstanden*," I answered.

Our bilingual conversation made our journey around countless roundabouts memorable. Very gently, he spoke of the war that had ended just ten years earlier. He told me he was a fabric manufacturer in Leeds and had served as an infantry officer at the front.

"May I ask you how you felt about us Germans as a people then?" I questioned him.

"Naturally, I despised Hitler, the Nazis and their fellow-travelers," he said. "But I had met so many marvelous Germans when I was young that I could not hate all 85 million of you. Moreover, I was embarrassed by the destruction we wrought and felt sorry for the women and children killed in our air war."

Halfway along the Great North Road, we stopped for lunch in an ancient pub where he introduced me to steak-and-kidney pie, a dish consisting of diced beef, diced kidneys, onions, and gravy served in a pastry shell. Steak-and-kidney pie has since been my favorite food in Britain, surpassed only by roast partridge, to which I was introduced decades later in the Connaught Hotel in London.

After many hours on the Great North Road, my benefactor stopped at the junction with the A-64.

"This will be the end of our journey together, I'm afraid," he said. "I shall have to turn left to Leeds, and you must go right to York. Over there is a bus stop. Don't hitchhike today anymore, I beg you. It will be getting dark soon. A coach should be here soon. Take it! Can you pay for the fare?"

"Yes, thanks!" I answered, knowing I had a 5-pound note at the bottom of the right pocket of my Loden coat.

"Very well," he said, patting my coat just about at the place where the fiver was stored.

Crossing the A-1 diagonally, I reached into my right pocket to get out my five-pound note to pay for my bus fare. I found not one, but two fivers, one of which my host had slipped there unnoticed.

After a few minutes, the double-decker bus to York arrived. I paid my fare. "Half a crown," the conductor said. I handed him one of my fivers and received a fistful of banknotes and coins in return. I climbed upstairs, sat next to a young man about my age, and studied the bewildering British currency in my hand. It seemed so weird, so hugely different from the decimal system in Germany, that I asked my neighbor to explain it to me.

"I know this is puzzling to foreigners," he said. "Let's begin with a farthing, which is not much used anymore; the farthing is a quarter penny. Then comes the ha'penny (a half penny), here is one. What follows is the penny, a rather absurd coin; it is so heavy that it makes holes in your trouser pockets. Next, we have this copper-colored thing with twelve corners. We call it a thruppence (three pennies). Then we have this coin here, a sixpence. What follows is the bob, or shilling, the equivalent of 12 pence. Here is one. They are often hard to come by, especially when you need them for your electric heater, which is the case most of the year. Then there is the half crown, another heavy bugger. That's the end of the coins."

"And what comes after that?"

"The ten-bob-note, ten shillings to you, and finally the pound, equaling 20 shillings. We call it quid."

"Phew!"

"That's not all! When you buy a suit or an overcoat or rent a flat, your price will be quoted in guineas, but there is no guinea note or coin," he went on.

"So, what do you pay when ordering a new suit? Nothing?"

"No, you pay one quid and one bob, and that's a guinea."

"This all sounds a little wacky," I said.

"If you think so," he replied, slightly miffed.

"My name is Uwe," I said, giving him my hand.

"I am Archibald," he answered. We became friends. The next morning, he picked me up at the youth hostel to show me his hometown. We walked back into the city center and halted before the massive York Minster, Europe's biggest gothic cathedral.

"What a splendid church this is!" I exclaimed.

"Let's go to Evensong."

"Let's!"

As I regaled in the most memorable church service of my year in England, I wondered if such splendor would be truly eternal or if it would not turn out to be ephemeral, like the British Empire, which was collapsing. I dismissed this latter thought as preposterous but stood corrected almost three decades later by an event resembling Old Testament accounts of the wrath of God.

On the 6th of July 1984, David Jenkins, an irritatingly liberal theologian who questioned basic Christian tenets such as Christ's virgin birth and bodily resurrection, was consecrated bishop of Durham in York Minster, despite the fierce protests of clerics and thousands of lay people from his diocese.

Three days later, a thunderbolt struck the cathedral's south transept, causing huge damage, which made even the secular press wonder whether this was an act of a wrathful God.

I had still not reached Melbourne, an East Yorkshire farming village that was my final destination. Nearby, a former POW camp of Nissen huts had been converted to house foreign volunteer agricultural workers, mostly students striving to improve their English while working in fields or orchards. Next to the camp was an old Royal Air

Force base with long-abandoned buildings harboring merrymakers whose lusty activities were not countenanced inside the corrugated iron lodgings where the foreigners slept.

The bus from York to Melbourne took 20 minutes. It stopped outside The Cross Keys, a pub since renamed The Melbourne Arms. It was Sunday lunchtime.

As I entered, I heard an inebriated chorus of females chanting:

Maybe it's because I'm a Londoner
That I love London SOOO-ow
Well, maybe it's because I'm a Londoner
That I think of her wherever I go.

I get a funny feeling inside of me,
While walking up and down.
Well, maybe it's because I'm a Londoner
That I love the London town ...

This sparked my curiosity. What was this ode to London all about—here, in the Northeast of England? And what was the strange accent in which these ladies sang? It reminded me of the idiom of working-class Berliners. "We are Cockneys!" The five young women sitting with one young man at a big round table to the left of the entrance enlightened me. They each had a pint of cider in front of them. The women introduced themselves. They were Pat and Pam, Brenda, Pauline, and Eileen. The young man's name was Harald,[1] Pauline's German boyfriend.

---

1 Name changed by the author.

Eileen was the most mature of the group, a shapely woman nearly 20 years my senior. She beckoned me to sit next to her, stroked my Loden coat, and whispered into my right ear, "This will make a cozy padding for the dusty floors of the RAF buildings."

"Please explain."

"You'll find out."

And I did in the evening of the next day when she guided me into a dusty RAF hut after eight hours of fieldwork and dinner in the camp canteen. Eileen solved the riddle of why all these London girls had moved into Nissen huts and frequented this particular village pub east of York.

"Well, love, the word's out in East London that exotic foreigners can be found down here[2] in Melbourne. Some of the girls were hoping for Italians but there aren't many of those in the camp. For me, a young German will do very well." That said, given the grueling nature of our labor, it was not easy to accommodate these lively ladies; we were exhausted.

We rose every morning at 6:00 a.m., showered, had breakfast, and boarded a rusty pre-war Bedford bus that took us to work, which in April was backbreaking, being the season that strawberries, new potatoes, or cabbage had to be picked. This involved bending down for eight hours every day. April was also the season of harvesting winter wheat, which involved yanking straw bales onto tractor-drawn trailers. For this, we were rewarded with the minimum wage of one pound, two shillings, and sixpence a day. Considering that food and lodging cost five pounds a week, we weren't left with much cash to

---

2 Yorkshire is in the North; in any other country, it would logically be located "up" and not "down." In England, one travels "up to London," even if you go there from the furthest point north, by the same token, one drives "down to York." As New Yorkers would say, "go figure ..."

take Cockney girls to the Cross Keys. Hence, our income had to be improved, which happened swiftly.

The English laborers picking potatoes or clearing the wheat fields with us turned out to be bone-idle. They only shone in trying to prevent us from working at a reasonable pace. Soon, they began sabotaging us. When we lifted the bales of straw with pitchforks on a trailer, a Yorkshireman on top of it threw the bundle of straw off to the opposite side. Luckily, the farmer's foreman saw this, reported it to his boss, and suggested that local and foreign laborers be assigned separate fields. Moreover, we aliens were allowed to do piece work, thus nearly doubling our income.

Now we could splash in the Cross Keys, though no longer on Pat, Pam, Brenda, Pauline, and Eileen, because they had only come to Melbourne for one week and were replaced by a new bunch of London girls, including one I found most enthralling. She was my age had olive-colored skin, thick, shiny black hair, black eyes, and curvaceous lips. Her mother was English, but her father was a Turkish Cypriot, and her name was Dilay, meaning Gorgeous Moon.

A week after Gorgeous Moon had gone home, Harald and I visited her and Pauline in London. After work on Friday, we took a bus to the Great North Road and then hitchhiked south, which was a strenuous undertaking. Not that it was hard to get a lift; British Road Services truck drivers were all too eager to invite us into the cabins of their red lorries, for they needed company to keep them awake on their long journey at a top speed of 30 miles per hour.

These lumbering vehicles were tools of torment. Their diesel engines were inside the driver's cabin. Harald and I took two-hour turns, one sleeping in the co-driver seat and the other roasting his rear on top of the motor, regaling the trucker with jolly tales. The driver rewarded us with a meal in a roadside café somewhere south of Doncaster, introducing us to the joys of baked beans on toast in addition to eggs, bacon, fried tomatoes, and toast.

"What are you going to the London area for?" asked the driver.

"Visiting our girlfriends," Harald answered. "Mine lives in the East End, and my friend's in Dulwich. But they are late risers. So, we won't see them until the early afternoon."

"And till then?"

"Washing ourselves and changing clothes in a public lavatory at Piccadilly Circus," I said.

"Don't!" warned the trucker.

"Why?"

"This is a cottage!"

"A cottage?"

"That's the nickname for public lavatories where homosexual men seek anonymous sex."

"In a men's room?" countered Harald incredulously.

"Yes, men with men."

"Yikes!"

"You said it!"

"Here's what you should do," the lorry driver continued. "Only a few steps from Piccadilly, you will find the oldest Lyons' Corner House. This is a beautiful old chain restaurant that is quite inexpensive. It has a clean lavatory where you can clean yourself up and change in safety."

He dropped us off at a London Transport stop, where we took a bus to Piccadilly. We walked around for an hour until the Lyons'

Corner House opened. It was beautiful; a waiter informed us it was pure Art Deco style.

"We have hitchhiked here from Yorkshire. Where may we wash and change before breakfast?" we asked him as we entered the restaurant. He directed us to the men's room.

"Please tell us about this lovely restaurant," we asked him when we came out.

"It is London's first teashop, founded in 1894 by Sir Joseph Lyons. What are you doing here? You look tired?"

"Visiting our girlfriends. We have just arrived from East Yorkshire."

"I suppose you need rest after breakfast."

"Indeed, but how?"

"Quite near here is a comfortable cinema that will open soon. Daytime shows are cheap. You can see two films for one ticket. You could sleep through the first film and enjoy the second, or vice versa."

We followed his advice and called our girlfriends after the second show.

"Where are you?" asked Gorgeous Moon's father, who had a slight Turkish accent. "Dilay has told us a lot about you and said you were coming today. Hurry! Lunch is getting cold. You can stay in our house—we have a spare room for you."

I was fed northern Cypriot dishes I had never tasted before, starting with meze, which included oil-soaked olives, grilled halloumi cheese, seasoned yogurts, charcoal-grilled meat, and assorted vegetables.

After the meal, he beckoned me to his garden whilst Dilay and her mother cleared the dining table.

"Uwe, we are worried about Dilay; perhaps you can help. She seems fond of you, and that's good."

"What worries you?"

"You see, she has a very nice job as a typist in the Air Ministry. She is only eighteen. If she stays there, she will advance. Try to persuade her to do that, please, Uwe!"

"Does she have other plans?"

"She has an incomprehensible obsession with snakes and wants to study them in South America."

"Snakes?"

"Yes, snakes! Don't ask me what this is all about!"

Hand in hand, Gorgeous Moon and I walked through Hyde Park.

"Dilay," I asked her, "Your father told me about your fascination with snakes."

"Yes, anacondas—green anacondas, to be precise."

"What do you want to do with green anacondas?"

"Nothing. I want an anaconda to do something for me."

"What on earth can a green anaconda do for you?"

"Eat me."

"You are jesting, Dilay, aren't you?" I said, shuddering when I saw how serious she was.

"Not at all. This has been my childhood dream. I am saving my money to travel to South America."

"And why does the snake have to be green?"

"Because green anacondas are so big that they can sometimes eat people, not often, but once in a while."

When evening came, she asked, "Do you like jazz? There is a marvelous new place in Coventry Street called Flamingo Jazz Club. It remains open until six in the morning." We jived feverishly that night; we embraced and exchanged hot kisses; we spoke little except about our love for each other. Green anacondas had ceased to be the topic. I was relieved.

At four in the afternoon, we came home. Gorgeous Moon's father received us at the door. I feared a paternal dressing down, but he laughed, pointing at the lipstick marks around my mouth.

"It is nice to see young people enjoying themselves." He sent Gorgeous Moon to her room and guided me to mine.

"Keep it up," he implored me, giving me a hug.

"I'll be back next Saturday," I promised.

"Oh, thank you, thank you. Good night!"

As arranged, I met Harald at the Mill Hill roundabout at 6:00 p.m. We were both in a merry mood, in love, well-fed, and determined to return to London the following weekend.

"I think I might marry Pauline," he revealed to me.

"For us, this would be a little early," I told him. "We are too young."

This trip turned out to be lucky for us. We had barely thumbed for two minutes when a blue Ford Zephyr stopped.

"Where are you going?" asked a young man in his late twenties.

"Melbourne, a village near York," said I.

"Where exactly?"

"We live in the former POW camp in Melbourne."

"Gosh, I know it—lots of Nissen huts. My home is only a few miles from there. I'll drop you off."

"Are you going to London often?"

"Yes, every weekend. My girlfriend works in London."

"We also have girlfriends in London; will you take us with you next Friday, please?"

"Of course, that will be fun. I'll pick you up at 7:00 p.m."

The following Friday, we arrived at 11:00 p.m. in Dulwich. Gorgeous Moon's father was still up. He seemed despondent.

"Don't expect much joy from Dilay. She is in a sour mood," he whispered. "All week, she has been begging me to buy her a ticket to Guyana," he continued, shaking his head. Guyana, a habitat of green anacondas, was then a British colony in the northeast of South America.

Gorgeous Moon, the same Gorgeous Moon who had kissed and cuddled me with such passion the week before, showed little interest in my arrival. Her father tried to reassure me: "Perhaps she'll be nicer tomorrow."

She wasn't. She acknowledged my presence at breakfast with a scant smile, did not speak a word to her parents, and vanished into her bedroom immediately after the meal.

"May I join you?" I asked her.

"Suit yourself. The door is open."

"Let's go for a walk, Dilay," I said.

"It's raining."

"Does it matter?"

"Yes, when I am bad-tempered, rain does matter. It would make me even more ill-tempered."

"With me?"

"Of course not," Gorgeous Moon replied. "I am cross with my father, who has plenty of money—"

"but he doesn't want you to go to South America," I completed her sentence. "Am I right, Dilay?"

She nodded.

"Well, don't take it amiss, Dilay, but, like your father, I don't want you to go into the jungle and feed yourself to a green anaconda. We both want you to live because we love you!"

"Get out of my room!"

By the early evening, her mood had not softened, and I decided to go sightseeing the next morning. Gorgeous Moon's father accompanied me to the door with tears in his eyes.

When I arrived in London one week later, Gorgeous Moon was no longer home.

"We have had to put her into a mental clinic," her father informed me.

"May I visit her?"

"No, visitors other than her parents are not allowed for the time being," he said.

Four years later, I came to London as an Associated Press reporter for a brief stint. I rushed to Gorgeous Moon's home in Dulwich, but it was sold.

"They have moved back to Northern Cyprus," a neighbor told me.

"Dilay, too?" I asked.

"No, she is somewhere else. I don't know where. Why not check with the Air Ministry?" said the neighbor.

The next morning, I called the ministry and reached a typist who had been Gorgeous Moon's friend.

"Dilay is no longer here," she said with a sigh. "All we know is that she has moved to South America. We never heard from her again."

But let's return to 1955. My bizarre experience with Gorgeous Moon dulled my interest in London girls for a while. Moreover, when Harald and I returned to Melbourne, we learned that there would be no work for us in that area and that we were to report to a large farm near Hull in two weeks' time.

"Let's take a little holiday in Edinburgh," I suggested to Harald.

"Let's do that!" he said. We hitchhiked in glorious weather and stayed in a rented caravan on a campground south of the Scottish capital, which we explored on the pillion seats of two BMW motorbikes belonging to a couple of cheerful Cologne girls, one with a wooden leg, which by no means lessened my interest in her.

The girls drove us south to the Hull hinterland, where, for me, the most enchanting phase of my year in England began. For reasons of privacy, I am withholding the names of the farm to which we were assigned and of its owner, his wife, and his comely daughter; my readers will understand as my tale unfolds. Let's call them Cuthbert, Helen, and Fiona. Fiona was my age, a strapping, healthy-looking girl with beautiful blue, smiling eyes, rosy cheeks, and, most importantly, a warm interest in me.

Early in August, we arrived at this magnificent estate with a splendid manor house, a family chapel, and a stable full of fur-footed heavy horses. Harald and I were lodged and fed in the estate manager's cottage. We were assigned to making hay, repairing dikes, looking after the chickens, and fixing one of their coops after I had crushed it by backing a tractor into it, which Cuthbert ignored while observing benignly Fiona's and my blossoming flirtation.

Cuthbert called me off the field one morning and said, "Come with me, lad."

I followed him to the attic of his manor house, where he unwrapped the dinner jacket he had worn when he was my age.

"Try this on, lad!" he told me. It fit.

"Good, I'll take it to the cleaners in Hull today. It will be ready for Friday when I'll take you out, my lad."

On Friday, he gave me the cleaned tuxedo, a wing-collar shirt, a black bow tie, black socks, and patent leather shoes. "Put these on, and I'll pick you up at five. We are going to the Grand Hotel in Scarborough."

Thus far, I had seen Cuthbert rattle about his farm in a Land Rover. This time, he pulled up outside the estate manager's cottage in a Humber Pullman with a remarkably long snout and red leather seats. Helen sat by his side, and Fiona was in the back, giving me a sweet smile. As the Humber Pullman's six-cylinder engine purred through the lovely East Yorkshire countryside, Cuthbert regaled us with tales about our destination.

"The Grand Hotel is the second-most elegant establishment of its kind in the British countryside, surpassed only by the Imperial in Torquay in Devon," he explained. "It is nearly one hundred years old and has a splendid restaurant and wine cellar."

The Hotel towered over Scarborough, an old spa on the North Sea, according to Cuthbert. "Despite the deplorable weather, Scarborough competes with Baden-Baden in Germany and Vichy in France in being the leading thermal spa in Europe," he said. "We Yorkshiremen claim that the tradition of 'taking the waters' began here, although this tale might be a little fanciful."

"How did this come about?"

"The story goes that, in the 17th century, two distinguished local ladies went for a walk on the beach and saw brownish water bubbling out of the sand. They dipped their forefingers into it and found it tasted bitter. In those days, anything liquid, brown, and bitter was considered good for one's health, notably as a remedy against gout. The news of this discovery spread rapidly around the country, and soon enough, well-to-do ladies and gentlemen undertook long and arduous journeys from all corners of the kingdom to spend rainy days at the beach drinking brown and bitter water," said Cuthbert, chuckling.

"Are we going to have a sip of it too?" I asked.

"Jolly well not!" Cuthbert answered with a laugh. "We'll have a very fine pre-war claret."

"Claret?"

"Bordeaux wine," he translated. "To be precise, we shall have a bottle of Château Margaux, my favorite red wine; it is the finest from the Médoc region outside Bordeaux."

By now, we had arrived at the Grand Hotel and had been guided to our table, which afforded us a view of the grey North Sea. Cuthbert ordered four glasses of champagne as we studied the menu.

"Don't order fish as your main course," Cuthbert advised us. "A great claret must accompany red meat."

"That suits me. I am allergic to fish," I said.

"Bravo!"

When the meal was almost over, and the ladies had gone to "powder our noses," as Helen called it, Cuthbert offered me a glass of old port with which to finish my Wensley cheese (a Yorkshire delicacy), put on a broad grin, and said,

"Now, Uwe, as I gather from the state of my haystacks, you like my daughter."

I turned red.

"Don't be embarrassed. I enjoy watching your romance grow."

"Thank you, Cuthbert."

"Now, we Yorkshiremen and you Germans have quite a few things in common—for example, our candor."

"True!"

"So, let me be straightforward: How would you like to become a Yorkshire farmer?"

I stared at him, dumbfounded.

"I know you are a city boy with another future in mind," Cuthbert continued. "Have you any career plans?"

"Yes, I would like to become a journalist or caricaturist."

"But you seem to enjoy and like agricultural work, am I wrong?"

"No. I love it here."

"Let me explain to you what this little talk of ours is all about: My son died in the war. Somebody has to continue running this farm when I am old or gone. Fiona could not do this by herself. You two seem such a good match. If you agree, I shall send you to the Royal Agricultural College in Cirencester and then teach you how to run my estate."

"Cuthbert, I am speechless. You lost your son in a war against Germany, and now you ask a German to be your son?"

"Uwe, the war is over. My son died fighting Hitler, not you. I am a Christian and therefore love you as a child of God."

Cuthbert saw that I was wrestling with a dilemma. On the one hand, his offer revealed the most beautiful Christian frame of mind, and I loved Fiona. On the other hand, I felt too young and immature to commit myself.

Cuthbert sensed my hesitations.

"Don't worry, my lad, I won't pressure you. Take your time, think it over."

But I did worry, brooding about his offer for three weeks. In the end, though, my spirit of adventure prevailed, and I apprised Cuthbert, Helen, and Fiona of my decision as gently as possible. Fiona stared at me with sadness. Cuthbert said warmly, "I wish you God's blessing." Helen nodded.

Almost thirty years later, I stayed with my friend Henry, the Eighth Earl Bathurst, in his manor in Cirencester, where Henry had been governor of the Royal Agricultural College. I told him about Fiona and Cuthbert and how he had almost sent me to this school to then run his estate.

"Can you believe it, Henry?" I asked. "This marvelous man wanted me to marry Fiona. He wanted me, a German, to marry his daughter and replace his son, who had died in the war. This was the most moving thing anybody has ever said to me! For thirty years now, I have often felt guilty for letting him and Fiona down, although I am grateful to have married an Englishwoman much like her: jolly, humorous, bouncy, and rosy-cheeked. I wonder what's happened to them."

"Go and find out," Henry said, "Take my Vauxhall Estate and drive to Yorkshire." I did the following day. What I discovered depressed me. Cuthbert's once elegant house was empty and seemed in a state of decay, as was his chapel, where grass and even trees were growing out of the roof. The stable that used to house a host of heavy horses had lost its roof. I went to the village pub to ask about Cuthbert's family. A few old codgers remembered them. They told me he had given up his farm long ago but had no idea where he, Helen, and Fiona had ended up.

Full of remorse, I drove back to Cirencester.

In 1955, I spent another few days on Cuthbert's estate, after which the National Farmers' Union assigned Harald and me once again to a former POW camp. This one was located in Friday Bridge near Wisbech in Cambridgeshire. No sooner did we arrive than BBC television broadcast live the arrival of the last German prisoners of war from the Soviet Union. When the camera focused on one particular railway car and showed the first POW get off the train, Harald shouted, "There is my father!"

Harald was on his way home the next day, and I had lost my companion just as the funniest episode of my year in England commenced. The inmates of the Volunteer Agricultural Camp Friday Bridge were first assigned to potato fields and subsequently to canneries in the Wisbech area, where some of us were ordered to improve the color and taste of peas and strawberries. Incongruously, the factories had boiled both out of vegetables and fruit to make them fit for canning. Their lack of pigments made them look like athlete's foot, and I dared not try their taste.

The foreman handed me a shovel and sent me to the inter-floor level halfway between the ceiling and a conveyor belt filled with open cans containing the non-descript substance. There was a hole with a funnel pointing to the cans. Around the hole, four conical piles of powder were neatly assembled, one red, one green, and two white, the latter being sugar and salt. As the conveyor belt began moving, making the tins rattle merrily, the foreman shouted, "Peas!" This was my order to dump two shovels of green powder and just a bit of salt into the funnel every minute or until the foreman, shouting "Whoa," commanded me to stop.

Next, he screamed, "strawbugs," meaning strawberries, and I had to repeat the same procedure, except with red powder and sugar.

This assignment was so hilarious that we foreign workers conspired to color some peas red, make them taste sweet, and some strawberries green and flavor them with salt. Nobody at the cannery noticed, but we regaled in anticipated schadenfreude, thinking about shoppers who, many years hence, would load sweet red peas or salty green strawberries on their plates.

It was early December, and it was time to return to Germany to spend Christmas with my mother. Hitchhiking in the winter was no joy, but I received wise counsel from the German lecturer who had chided me in the London youth hostel for sewing our national flag on my rucksack and whom I had met again in the Friday Bridge camp.

"Why don't you try to get a lift on a freighter?" he suggested.

"Does that work?"

"How do you think I got here from Pakistan? On freighters!"

"Where do I board?"

"Boston in Lincolnshire, interesting town. In the Middle Ages, the Hanseatic League ranked it an important port for trade with continental Europe."

So, I hitchhiked to the Boston inland port where, on a canal leading to the North Sea, a small freighter named *Erika Hendrik Visser* was moored; it was registered in Cologne on the Rhine, not far from Hagen, where my mother lived.

"Are you going to Cologne?" I asked a red-nosed merchant marine officer swaying up and down beside the ship. He had three stripes on his sleeves, indicating he was the first officer.

"We are only registered in Cologne but never go up the Rhine," he replied.

"But are you going anywhere in Germany, then?"

"Well, our final destination will be the Soviet Union, but we will first stop in Brunsbüttel, the western entrance of the Kiel Canal in Germany."

"Can you take me, please?"

"Sure, come aboard, go amidships where you'll find a door marked by a red cross. That's our sickbay. It's empty. You can sleep there. We're leaving soon. I'll meet you in the officers' mess for dinner."

I did as he told me, dumped my rucksack in the sickbay, cleaned up, and went to the dining room. Minutes later, another officer with four stripes on his sleeves arrived and sat beside me. He was the captain and seemed at first preoccupied with the worsening weather; the Erika Hendrik Visser had left the dock and was well on its way to the North Sea.

Suddenly, he noticed me.

"*Wer, zum Teufel, bist Du* (Who the hell are you)?"

"Uwe Siemon-Netto."

"What are you doing here?"

"Traveling to Brunsbüttelkoog."

"Who allowed you on board?"

"This gentleman," I said, pointing at the first officer, who was lolling in his chair opposite the captain.

"But this is against the rules of the Visser shipping company." Turning to the second officer, he asked, "Can we turn back?"

"Impossible. We have almost reached the North Sea."

"Do you have papers?" the captain asked me.

"My passport."

"I didn't mean that. Do you have a seaman's license or insurance, that kind of thing?"

"No."

The captain went puce in the face.

"I'll have no choice. I must let you stay on board until Brunsbüttel but don't think I will let you travel for free. Get me cookie!" The cook appeared in the officers' mess.

"Yes, Captain?"

"Take this good-for-nothing urchin and make him work. Let him peel the potatoes, serve meals, wash the dishes!"

"Yes, Captain!"

I was quite happy working in the galley. Eventually, the cook sent me to bed and ordered me to return at 5:00 a.m. to prepare breakfast.

When I woke, a fierce storm shook the ship about. I began feeling woozy in the stomach but remembered what the lecturer from Peshawar had told me in the Friday Bridge camp: "When you are beginning to feel seasick, eat a big chunk of bacon, then a thick slice of black bread, and wash it down with a huge *Schluck* (gulp) of *Korn* (a white Schnapps).[3] This will make you puke, after which you'll be fine." I went into the galley. Cookie was absent, but I found everything I needed, ate, drank, vomited down the staircase into the engine room, and felt chipper.

Then, I peeked into the officer's mess and saw the captain sitting by himself. I made his breakfast and served him.

"How come you aren't green in the face?" he asked. I told him about the lecturer's recipe.

"Respect! You and I seem to be the only people on this vessel who know this trick."

---

3 Germans call all forms of hard liquor, such as gin, vodka, corn or fruit brandy, *Schnapps*. Not sweet alcoholic drinks, though; they are called *Likör*.

From then on, we were friends. When we docked in Brunsbüttel, the captain said, "If you would like to stay on board, I could get you a seaman's license and hire you as a trainee."

"Thanks, Captain, but I want to spend Christmas with my mother."

"You could meet us at the port of Frederikshavn in Denmark, where we will be docked during Christmas. I'll have your papers ready. What do you plan to do after the holidays?"

"On the first of January, I shall be hitchhiking to Paris."

CHAPTER 9

Urchin in Paris

MY JOURNEY TO PARIS began not as well as my trip to England, but my first stint in France turned out to be rich in beautiful experiences. I left home in Hagen with 70 DM in my pocket, equaling less than 20 U.S. dollars, which was all Mutti could spare. My father's Christmas letter was noteworthy for its unseasonal dearth of kindness. It started out commending me grudgingly for my stay in England, where I had worked for my living. This appealed to his fervent Anglophilia. But France? Did I not know how much he hated the French after he, a blinded German soldier, had been so horribly mistreated in their POW camp in World War I? No, no, no! I shouldn't count even on pocket money from him as I am "bumming around Paris," as Vati phrased it. All he was prepared to pay was my compulsory alimony, but Mutti needed that money to run our household in Hagen. Vati deeply resented this. He hated her because she had dropped him, an eyeless man.

In retrospect, it was reckless of me to set off for Paris in the middle of the winter without any job prospects in the capital of a country that, to us Germans, had been the archenemy a decade ago. Moreover, I didn't leave on a balmy spring day like the year before when I went to England. It was freezing when I began hitchhiking west at eight in the morning on January 1, 1956, and trying to get a lift proved a stop-and-go undertaking. Sometimes, a driver took me just ten or fifteen kilometers before depositing me somewhere in the gritty Ruhr District, where I then stood shivering for an hour or more until another charitable soul picked me up for another short stretch.

It took sixteen lifts to reach a nondescript town somewhere near Mons in the French-speaking part of Belgium late in the evening, and then my voyage ground to a halt. I had finished the liverwurst sandwiches and emptied the hot cocoa from the thermos flask Mutti had packed into my rucksack. Now, it was pitch dark; not a single car or truck came by. The cozy duffle coat I had bought in Boston, East Anglia, before leaving England on the rusty freighter *Erika Hendrik Visser* could no longer keep me warm. I began to cry but pulled myself together quickly.

I walked around the town and found no sign of an open hotel, much less a youth hostel, but discovered two blue lanterns with the white letters "Police" and "*Politie*," the latter being Flemish (Dutch). By now, it was eleven o'clock. Desperate, I walked into the station and told the fatherly duty sergeant my tale of woe.

"Would you know where I might find a warm place to spend the night?" I asked him.

"No, I can't, young man. On the other hand, it would be irresponsible of me to send you out into the cold again. You wouldn't survive the night."

"May I just sit here and stay warm?" I pleaded.

"I have a better idea. You can stay in a cell. It's heated and has a bunk bed with a blanket, a wash basin, and a latrine. I won't lock you in. *Tu es un jeune homme courageux* (you are a brave young fellow). Sleep well. I'll bring you breakfast in the morning."

Thus, I spent a night in jail for the first time in my life,[1] but was I ever grateful! I have slept in some of the world's most luxurious hotels since, but nowhere better than that night in the clink. Early in the morning, the kindly police sergeant served me a tray of bread rolls with butter and jam, an apple, and sweet café au lait. Like my mother the day before, he placed a pack of sandwiches in my rucksack.

"Try to be ready in one hour. When my shift is over, I'll drive you to the edge of town, where you might get a lift to Paris more easily."

This enchanting episode has shaped my opinion of cops for the rest of my life. I could never join the chorus of rebellious morons calling all policemen pigs in America and *Bullen* (bulls) in Germany during the student revolts of the nineteen-sixties. In my head, the image of a decent law enforcement officer was cast forever by this sergeant in a one-horse town somewhere in Belgium.

That said, my ongoing journey began as drearily as the day before: ten kilometers, twenty kilometers, five kilometers, and then forty by truck. It was two in the afternoon when I reached the French border, where an immigration officer gave me an invaluable tip:

"If you want to get to Paris in one fell swoop, ask drivers of vehicles whose license plates end with the number "75," indicating that they are registered in the *Département Seine-St. Dénis*, which includes the capital. Everybody must stop here, so that's your best bet of getting a lift. In fact, here's one now!"

A black Citroën 11CV stopped in front of us, one of the most elegant, mass-produced cars ever, commonly known as a *Traction Avant* (front-wheel drive). It had a "75" on its license plate. As the driver

---

1 I was incarcerated in a Stasi jail in East Berlin for two days five years after this, but this story will be told later.

flashed his passport to the officer, I asked if he would take me to Paris. "Get in," he said cheerfully.

The driver was a gentleman in his mid-thirties with a leaden right foot. There was no *autoroute* (freeway) connecting Belgium and France; that came much later. But there was a wide *route nationale*, allowing my benefactor to get the most out of his six-cylinder engine. He was a vivid conversationalist, in such a jolly mood that I dared to ask him what made him so happy.

"Ah, *jeune homme* (young man), I had such a memorable stay in Brussels. I have two reasons for feeling so elated. First, I spent the holidays in the arms of the most elegant lady I have ever met, and second, I learned a lot of details about plans to make Brussels the capital of the European Economic Community (EEC), which should come into being in two years time. Do you know what this is all about?"

"Only vaguely," I answered, "but tell me more."

"If all goes well, the EEC will eventually evolve into a European Union, following the plans of the saintly Robert Schuman (a French government minister born in Luxembourg), your Chancellor Konrad Adenauer, and others. If you have been through the last war, you will understand how much I rejoice over this development. Where were you in the war?"

"In Leipzig," I said.

"Being bombed?"

"Yes."

"I can imagine it was hell."

"It was, but I survived. Where were you?"

"I am a Parisian, but my family spent these years in our country home in Free France, as the unoccupied part of our nation was called. Anyway, all this is all over: the war, the occupation, the rancor. Now, we can look forward to a united Europe. I am a journalist. When I get to Paris, I will write a big series about this topic. I have done a lot of research in Brussels."

"Where? In the arms of your lady friend?" I asked facetiously.

He chuckled: "There is no better place to practice journalism than in a woman's warm arms."

This seemed logical to me.

"What are you going to be when you grow up?" he wanted to know.

"A journalist, if I can."

"I like to hear that."

"How did your romance help you in your assignment?"

"Ah, I forgot to tell you: She is a member of a small French foreign ministry delegation tasked to figure out whether Brussels will be the most suited venue for the European capital."

"Aha."

"Where are you going to stay in Paris?"

"No idea. I have very little money and must find a cheap room while looking for a job."

"I think I know the right place in my neighborhood. It's called Hôtel des Étrangers. Let me take you there."

The Hôtel des Étrangers[2] at 2 rue Racine, corner Boulevard St. Michel, in the Latin Quarter, was the perfect place. I was given a small attic room on the sixth (American: seventh) floor for 500 *anciens francs*[3]

---

2 Now called the Hôtel Belloy Saint-Germain.

3 In 1956, the currency today known as *ancien franc* was still legal tender in France. The exchange rate to the U.S. dollar was $1 = FRF 400. In 1960, the franc was revalued. From then on, FRF 100 equaled one *nouveau franc* (new franc). In 2002, the euro was introduced in 12 member states of the European Union, including France. Later, eight more acceded to the so-called Eurozone. At the time of conversion, the euro was worth 6.56 *nouveaux francs*.

($1.25), breakfast included. It was a modest chamber with a single bed, a table, a chair, a wash basin, a closet, and a lavatory directly next door. But from its window, I had a magnificent view over the roofs of Paris and of the Notre Dame cathedral.

The rent of $1.25 was peanuts, but not if one had a mere 70 DM in one's pocket. The kind-hearted hotel manager called his counterpart at a self-service restaurant on the other side of the Boulevard Saint-Michel, who hired me as a dishwasher and a gofer to take the garbage out and carry the groceries from his delivery van to his pantry. He paid me FRF 1,500 a day, three times my rent, and fed me a free meal. I was elated, but my bliss was quickly dampened by a radical Communist on the kitchen staff who reported me to his union, which in turn denounced me to the state labor and immigration authorities. Hence, on the sixth day, two stern-looking officials entered Le Self, as the French called these types of eateries, and arrested the manager and me, him for employing me without a work permit and me for working without such a certificate.

When I met the manager again after a week, he told me a truism I would hear many decades later in the United States: "No good deed goes unpunished. I received a stiff fine." I, on the other hand, was lucky. The two men, obviously anti-Communists, ushered me into a separate room, smiled, and whipped out two forms for me to fill out, one from the labor office and the other from Immigration, but both intended to put me on a fast track for being allowed to stay in France and perform lowly chores for my survival. It was clear that they enjoyed sticking it to the Communists, whom they thought had become far too powerful in France at that time. This eventually proved to be a blessing for me, though for the next two weeks, I felt I was being led through a dark tunnel, an experience teaching me what it was like to be a Paris *clochard*, a bum.

To save money, I moved to the Socialist youth hostel on Montmartre, which was a calamitous choice. There was only one other guest in my dorm, an Algerian with a hostile demeanor. In his north African country, which was part of France then, a brutal guerilla war of liberation was raging, and many Arabs in Paris hated all Europeans regardless of nationality. This Algerian who robbed me probably saw himself as a freedom fighter.

When I woke up in the morning, he was gone, as were my rucksack, my change of clothing, and the chest pouch with my money. Now, I was both penniless and homeless because I could no longer pay for my bed in the hostel. So, I wandered exhaustively from street to street and shop to shop, asking for work, but I had no success. It was getting dark when I arrived at the sanctuary of the Evangelical-Lutheran Free Church of Alsace-Lorraine. Next to it was the parsonage. On the ground floor, I spied the pastor working at his desk. I walked in, triggering the most un-Christian outburst I have ever witnessed in a man of the cloth. Our conversation went thus:

I (in French): "Good evening, Monsieur le Pasteur. I am a German and have just been robbed in the youth hostel. Do you know anybody in your congregation needing help with his business or at home?"

Pastor (puce in the face and with a thick German accent). "*Ah, le boche* (German blockhead, or Kraut)! First, you occupy our country, and now you come here, begging. Out! Out! Out!"

I (in French): "But pastor, I am not begging. I am just asking if anyone in your parish might have any work for me."

Pastor (even more puce in the face and now screaming): "I said, out!" With that, he shoved me violently out of the door.

And I swore to myself silently: "One day, I'll see to it that you will get your comeuppance."

Next, I tried the Salvation Army, hoping to find a bed for the night. A lieutenant explained to me that I had come to the wrong place.

"I am sorry, but this is the French Salvation Army's officers' academy. We have no room. But take this; it might buy you a little food," he said, handing me a 500-franc note ($1.25).

The evening ended on a happier note. I decided to try my luck with men I presumed to be the poorest of the poorest: long-haired, bearded *clochards* (bums) who huddled at night in the *métro* (subway) stations until the trains stopped running at midnight when they moved above ground to assemble around grills emitting warm air from the underground tubes.

The *clochards*, all much older than I, welcomed me warmly in their midst.

"What brings you here?" one asked in an astonishingly cultured voice.

"I was robbed in the socialist youth hostel and then kicked out by a Lutheran pastor when I asked him if some member of his parish might have work for me. He called me a *boche*."

"Who was that guy?"

"I didn't get his name, but he was the pastor of the Evangelical-Lutheran Free Church of Alsace-Lorraine. He had a thick German accent."

The bearded men nodded. "We have known him since the war. He was a real scumbag then. Now, he poses as a born-again member of the resistance. He is contemptible."

"He is."

They stared at me for a few minutes.

"You are not a *clochard*," the man with the cultured voice said. "You are just out of pocket."

"Yes."

"You are too young to live like us."

"Probably, but I like being with you."

"Maybe so," the man with the cultured voice continued. "But we don't want you to freeze with us." He turned to his neighbor, a tall, gentlemanly figure.

"Come on, Alexandre, give yourself a jolt."

"I will," Alexandre agreed, unscrewed his left leg, which was a wooden hollow prosthesis, and fished out an FRF 5,000 note ($12.59). "Go, find a hotel room, and meet us for lunch at the little convent in the Rue des Grands Augustins. You will find us there lining up for soup at 11:30 in the morning."

The man with the cultured voice rose and told his friends, "I'll accompany this kid for a few blocks to make sure he doesn't get robbed."

On the way to the exit of the *métro* station, I asked him, "Who is this gentleman who just gave me so much money? Doesn't he need it for himself?"

"He doesn't. He is a wealthy marquis who spends the summer on his estate in the countryside and half the week in the winter in his town-house in Paris. He likes our company. He says we're honest companions."

"Is he...?"

"What? *Une tapette* (a queer)? Oh no, not at all! He is just a very generous and witty man, well-educated like many of us. We like living the way we are."

He returned to his group. I checked into the Hôtel des Étrangers, where I was welcomed with big smiles. At 6:30 in the morning, the manager knocked at my door, bringing me a fresh shirt, socks, and underwear.

"Give me your laundry, and I'll have it washed for you," he said, "From what I hear, it is quite dirty and smelly. I can't let you go job-hunting that way. Here, take what I have brought you."

I joined a long queue of clochards lining up for soup outside the little convent in the narrow Rue des Grands Augustins. As I approached the door, a well-dressed lady came out and pulled me into her office.

"You are not a bum, are you?" she asked.

"No, I was robbed in a youth hostel," I answered.

She handed me an address and said, "Copy this in your handwriting."

I did, and she complimented me, "Pretty handwriting. Difficult to read but nice to look at. Let's see what I can do. Stay here and have something to eat. I will send this off by pneumatic tube[4], and I should get an answer in a few hours." She left her office for a few hours.

Late in the afternoon, she received the answer and was jubilant. "They accepted you!"

"Who accepted me?"

"Simca,[5] the car manufacturers. They are expecting you. They want you to be at their office on the Champs-Élysées tomorrow morning at eight."

"To do what?"

---

4 The French postal system owned an extensive network of pneumatic tubes through which mail was moved at very high speeds by air pressure around Paris. Its first line was built in 1866. Since 1984, the network is no longer available for private use.

5 *Société Industrielle de Mécanique et Carrosserie Automobile.*

"Write addresses on at least one thousand envelopes for invitations to their exhibit at the Paris Auto Show in April," the lady said.

"Don't they have typewriters?"

"Of course, they do. But French corporations prefer to send out handwritten envelopes for special occasions; they say it's more stylish. When this job is over, come back to see me. I'll find something else for you."

At eight o'clock sharp, I presented myself at Simca's offices. A secretary ushered me into a room overlooking the most elegant boulevard in Paris and gave me a huge box of envelopes, a long list of addresses, a simple fountain pen, and an inkwell.

"Start writing," she said, "We will pay you 20 francs per envelope.[6] I estimate that you will have at least three days' work here."

She was right. After three days, I had addressed 1,350 envelopes and was paid FRF 27,000 ($67.50), plus a bonus of FRF 3,000 ($7.50). I was happy, especially as the secretary brought me a baguette with butter, ham, cornichons, and sausage for lunch. I decided to rest my tired right hand and walk around the Latin Quarter for three days and dance every night in the Câveau de la Huchette, a Dixieland club, to the music of the clarinet genius Maxim Saury and his band, which turned out to be a challenge for my right hand because one evening just before midnight a gang of Algerians stormed the jazz cellar to beat up us revelers, mostly students, stabbing a few and giving me a black eye before the police came and packed the Arabs into their vans. Little did I know at the time that this was a mild foretaste of the guerilla war I was to cover as a reporter ten years later in Vietnam.

---

6 FRF 20 equaling $0.05.

"Whatever happened to you?" asked the lady in the Augustinian convent the next morning when I came to thank her for the Simca job and ask if she had more work for me.

I explained.

"How horrible! But I can't send you to places like the Champs-Élysées with a black eye like this. A couple of companies contacted me for temporary workers, but they wouldn't let someone looking like a violent thug across their doorstep."

"But I am not a thug, Madame!"

"I know, I know, but you look it. Don't worry. Let me make a call."

She dialed a number, described me and my black eye, and told her interlocuter my story. I heard him say, "Send him over."

She gave me a name, an address, and a telephone number. "That was Father Heinz Heger, the German Catholic chaplain in Paris. Go there now. He wants to see you urgently."

"Does he know that I am Lutheran, Madame?"

"He doesn't care as long as you are a Christian."

"Yes, Madame, I am."

She hugged me and sent me off.

Father Heger received me half an hour later in his parsonage. He was the exact opposite of the unpleasant Lutheran pastor who called me a *boche*.

"I am so grateful to the lady in the front office of the Augustinian convent. She sends me such nice young men for handyman jobs. The last one was an amiable boy but clumsy. The poor lad kept kicking over paint pots all the time. But never mind. He is about to enter a Trappist monastery in Germany anyway. Do you paint?"

"Yes, watercolors, some oils, and I do caricatures..."

"No, not that! I meant, can you paint walls?"

"I haven't done that yet. But there is no reason why I should not learn to paint walls quickly, considering that I have painted quite a few pictures."

"Let me make a call."

"*Bonjour mon frère* (brother)," he said, "I think I found the right young man for you...Yes?... Of course, I'll ask him before I send him over."

Turning to me, he said, "This was Frère Corona, the majordomo of the prefecture of the Christian Brothers, a congregation of Catholic teachers and librarians in the department of Paris-Saint-Dénis. There is an Italian painter in his friary who does its walls this winter. He needs an assistant, but the other German I recommended for this job wasn't much use. Frère Corona wants me to ask you: Are you a Christian?"

"Yes, but a Lutheran."

"A real, believing Lutheran or a nominal Lutheran?"

"A real Lutheran, catechized by my grandmother and confirmed by Pastor Johannes Kruse in Hagen-Emst."

"Dear friend," said Father Heger, "in this parish, we no longer distinguish between faithful Lutherans and faithful Catholics. People here have been through far too many horrors to harbor silly prejudices against fellow Christians. In the war, my predecessor, Abbé Franz Stock, was also appointed garrison chaplain by the Wehrmacht. In this position, he ministered to three Paris military prisons: Fresnes, La Santé, and Cherche Midi. He had to give pastoral care to 4,500 condemned convicts and accompany them to their execution."

Father Heger called Frère Corona again. "He is a practicing Lutheran...ah! That's fine?... Yes, I'll tell him."

He hung up and said, "You are hired. Go immediately to 78 rue de Sèvres. Ask for Frère Corona. Give him your Lutheran pastor's address. A German-speaking brother will write to him, but you can move in right away and begin work tomorrow morning. May the Lord bless you!"

Frère Corona was a chubby friar with a smiling red face.

"First, let me explain to you who we are. We are not priests but lay brothers who live together in a monastic setting but go to work every morning at Catholic schools in Paris. You will be living with us. Let me show you your room. This is where you will sleep. You will eat breakfast, lunch, and dinner with us. We'll do your laundry for you, and you will receive 2,000 francs ($5) pocket money per week. This evening, you will meet Alessandro, our Italian painter. But first, let me introduce you to our superior, the *frère directeur* (brother director)."

The frère directeur greeted me with a bemused smile. "Behold, a Lutheran! *Pecca fortiter sed fortius fide et gaude in Christo*," he said. "Can you translate this?"

"Sin boldly but even more boldly believe and rejoice in Christ. It's from Luther."

"I know, and I love it!"

"You look like a Lutheran pastor, too: black robe and white preaching tabs."

"I know, but we aren't preachers; we're teachers. Welcome to our home."

Just before supper, I met Alessandro, the painter.

"Can you paint walls?" he asked.

"I'll learn quickly if you will teach me."

"I will. Are you prepared to start work at four in the morning?"

"Yes, but why so early?"

"I spend every winter in this city with its many museums and exhibitions. What's the point of painting walls from nine to five and missing all this wealth of culture? No! We will begin at four, breakfast break at six-thirty and stop at twelve. Then we'll have lunch and spend the rest of the day wandering about town, *d'accord* (agreed)?"

"Will you take me with you?"

"Sometimes, not always. Most of the time I will meet with my lady friend. Then I prefer to be alone with her."

"I understand."

"What are your favorite forms of modern art?" he asked me.

"Post-Impressionism, Expressionism, Cubism, Surrealism."

"You'll find plenty of that in Paris."

He took me to many exhibitions, and when he couldn't, my new friend David Brown did. David was a classy black American from Los Angeles who spent half the year in Paris, where he felt more accepted as a man of color than in his hometown.

We met in the Câveau de la Huchette, where I no longer had to pay admission after receiving a black eye from the fight with those Algerian gang members whom we jazz fans prevented from absconding with our girls. One of these girls was Marianne Küchle, an exquisite blonde from Zürich. We fell in love after dancing closely to the blues.

"What is this hard thing in your right pocket?" she asked.

"It is the key to my monastery."

"What? Do you mean to tell me that I am dancing cheek-to-cheek with a monk?"

"No, I am just living in a monastery, painting its interior walls."

"Can you show it to me? It would be such fun!"

"I can take you to the convent's door and kiss you goodbye but not sneak you inside. That wouldn't be allowed."

"How very sensual to be embraced by the boy I love under the archway of his monastery, feeling the convent's key in his trouser pocket—and that in Paris of all places!"

"Come!"

We walked arm-in-arm late that night from the Latin Quarter to 78, Rue de Sèvres in the seventh arrondissement (district). We arrived at the door leading to the Christian Brothers' courtyard. We kissed passionately. She pulled the key out of my right pocket with a wicked smile.

"Open!" she commanded, "I just want to look inside."

I unlocked the door. All the windows were dark except one.

"Who is in there?" she whispered.

"The *frère directeur*, our boss."

"Ouch! I'd better leave quickly. *Gute Nacht* (good night)."

"*Gute Nacht, ich liebe Dich* (I love you)."

"*Ich liebe Dich auch* (I love you, too)," she answered, "*bis morgen* (till tomorrow)."

Marianne and I remained together until she returned to Switzerland and I to Germany, but then our friendship took a tragic turn. We wrote to each other every week. One day, though, I received a letter from Marianne's mother telling me that she had been diagnosed with bone tuberculosis. "Poor Marianne has to lie in a plaster cast, probably for several years," her mother wrote. From then on, I assured her every week in a letter of my love. Marianne did the same, dictating her love letters to her mother from her gypsum bed. It took her five years to recover. I drove to Zürich in my Citroën 2CV. Her parents welcomed me warmly and lodged me in their guest room, but Marianne seemed peculiar. Was she embarrassed by my poor man's jalopy?

We decided to go swimming. Hesitantly, she climbed into my *Ente* (duck), as we Germans called these droll vehicles. On the beach, her bikini covered her glorious figure, but only minimally. I tried to kiss her. She turned away.

"I love another man," she explained. "He drives a Ferrari."

The next morning, I drove on to Saint-Tropez on the Côte d'Azur.

But I have deviated from my narrative. At this point, I am still in Paris. The morning after kissing Marianne under his archway, the *frère directeur* beckoned me into his office.

"I saw you with a young lady last night," he said with a smile.

"I didn't bring her in, though," I replied.

"I know, I know. I noticed that, too. But I have something else to discuss with you."

"Yes?"

"We received a letter from your pastor in Germany affirming that you are a Christian."

"Yes?"

"But we never see you go to church on Sunday. Here is a list of Lutheran churches in Paris, one quite close to our house. Of course, you are also welcome in our chapel."

I skimmed the list and discovered that it was led by the congregation of the unpleasant Alsatian pastor who had kicked me out of his parsonage, calling me a begging *boche*.

"*Mon frère directeur*, I'll gladly attend your chapel regularly, but first, I must go here," I said, pointing at the name of the Alsatian Lutheran sanctuary. "I'll tell you why when it's over."

"Go ahead! I'm curious."

The next Sunday morning, I put on a crisply washed shirt with the only tie I had brought with me from Germany and dressed in a dark suit my mother had sent me from Hagen. I admired myself at length in the mirror on my closet door and found that I actually looked quite civilized. Then, I set off to sit face-to-face with the Alsatian cleric. With wicked anticipation, I chose a seat in a pew in a straight line of vision from the pulpit.

I waited feverishly for the moment when he would ascend the stairs to his pulpit to preach. His gaze fell on me. He tried to look away but kept staring at me. He looked to the right, up, down, and then back at me. Now, he began to stutter. He stuttered until the end of his homily. Sweat dripped from his forehead. I just sat there with a hard stare fixed at him. It was clear to me at that moment that revenge in the house of God was not particularly Christian, but I won't deny that I had a very good time, which I readily confessed to the *Frère directeur* two hours later. He burst out laughing and slapped his thighs, saying, "Well done, Uwe, well, well done! You are funny."

When the service was over, and the pastor bade farewell to the worshipers, he had no choice but to extend his very wet right hand to me also.

"*Wir kennen uns doch, nicht wahr* (we know each other, don't we)?" he stuttered, sweat now pouring from his forehead.

"Yes, I came to your parsonage door."

"You are looking well," he answered, "well-fed and well-dressed."

"Yes, thanks to the Catholic Brothers who gave me work, a room, food, and a little money without asking me my denomination or nationality. Adieu, Herr Pfarrer (God be with you, pastor).

From then on, I attended Vesper services and Sunday Mass at the Christian Brothers' chapel. Two weeks later, the *Frère directeur* called me again into his office.

"Uwe," he said, "all of us are satisfied with your work. In May, Alessandro will return to Italy. If you like, you can then do his job by yourself for a proper wage."

"How fabulous, thank you!"

This wasn't to happen, however. I received a letter from Herr Beckmann, the cultural editor of the *Westfalenpost* in Hagen. "I missed your pieces on modern art in the Karl-Ernst Osthaus Museum but had no idea where to find you," he wrote. "Then your mother came to my office to discuss one of her concerts with me. 'Where is Uwe?' I asked her. She gave me your address. Now I am writing to you with a proposal, which I have already discussed with our editor-in-chief."

He went on, "We have three openings for two-year internships at the *Westfalenpost*. Come home to Hagen, and let us test you. If you pass, you'll receive probably the most rigorous training in journalism anywhere in the state of North Rhine-Westphalia." A ticket for the train trip from Paris to Hagen accompanied the letter.

In those days, most West German journalists were trained by regional newspapers. The curriculum included courses in media law, research, elegant ways to formulate news items, reportages, feature stories, commentaries, and tongue-in-cheek annotations, but also headlines, subtitles, captions, and performing technical tasks, such as pagination.

His newspaper, Herr Beckmann wrote, currently had three intern positions open. Twenty young people had already applied, some with university degrees, others not even with high school diplomas. All would have to pass strict exams in three weeks' time.

"Are you interested?" Herr Beckmann asked.

Was I ever interested! David Brown, the black artist friend of mine from Los Angeles, accompanied me to the Gare du Nord. Before I boarded the night train to Cologne, he sang for me—with a wicked grin—a World War I song by Walter Donaldson, who composed it with returning American servicemen in mind: "How Ya Gonna Keep 'em Down on the Farm (After They've Seen Paree?)."

"You sod!" I thought, worried about the grueling exam I had to sit the next day. But I passed, along with two other candidates also born in Leipzig, which I thought only appropriate, given that on July 1, 1650, our hometown had spawned *Einkommende Zeitung* (Incoming News), the first daily newspaper in the world. This established a tradition of journalistic excellence in Leipzig, which only vanished with the Nazi dictatorship followed by communism. Many leading editors and reporters in West Germany were refugees from that city.

CHAPTER 10

Urchin's Descent from Paris to Olpe

ON MONDAY, APRIL 16, 1956, I boarded the yellow tram number 2 from Hagen to Hohenlimburg, then a small satellite town that has at least one claim to fame: On May 3, 1846, it hatched Wilhelm Böing (d. 1890), who emigrated to the United States and built a fortune from land, timber, and mineral rights. His son, William E. Boeing, founded the global aerospace company that still bears the family name.

From Hohenlimburg, I took the steam train to Iserlohn, a mid-sized city where in mid-April 1956, I was assigned as *Redaktionsvolontär* (editorial trainee), the lowliest creature in journalism, with a stipend of 150 DM ($37.50) per month. My father, finally pleased with my choice of a career, topped this miserable income with an equal amount. So, I had $70, most of which I gave to my mother for my rent and food. She gave me one mark to pay for my lunch in an Iserlohn butcher shop, usually a greasy soup with some bits of meat or a sausage.

On the train, I joined a group of six commuters who assembled every morning in the same third-class compartment with seats of wooden slats. Two, always sitting by the window, were wounded

World War II veterans: a Latin teacher at an Iserlohn Gymnasium (classical high school) and a senior official in city hall—the teacher had lost his right leg, the other man his left arm. Such pairs were a frequent sight on German railways so soon after the end of the war.

Then, there was a grouchy old lady on her way to her job in a grocery store. She never smiled nor greeted us, but she always chose our coupé where, most often, she faced a pretty but sad-looking girl. Why she never smiled, I never found out. And then there was Gerda, a buxom, rather common woman, who sought my attention from the first day. Gerda was in her mid-thirties, at an age when, as a consequence of the recent war, women had a hard time finding a male companion. So many were dead.

One day, I met Gerda on the train back to Hohenlimburg. When we arrived, she said,

"Let's have a drink together."

"Why not?" I answered. "There's a good pub near the station."

"Oh, no!" said Gerda, "Let's go to my home; I must feed my cat."

We entered her flat on the ground floor. It reeked of cat and cabbage. No sooner had the front door shut than Gerda frantically rolled up her sweater and pulled my head down to her ample bosom whilst shoving her hand down the front of my pants, in which Gerda's feline ward also took a weird interest. Panic-stricken, I freed myself from this libidinous woman, ran out of her house, and jumped on the tram home to Hagen. The next morning, Gerda sat in a different coupé.

This put an end to my excursion into the realm of intergenerational lust for some time; I was too immature for that and, besides, had more important things to accomplish. An internship at a good German newspaper resembled basic training in the army. Herr Künkler, my bureau chief, was a rigorous drill sergeant. At the time, I hated him for that; now, I am deeply grateful, realizing how many of my basic skills as a journalist I owe to this man who sacrificed much of his time and nerves to train me.

He said, "First, you must learn accuracy. The best way to do this is to edit the *Gottesdienstordnung der Gemeinden* (service order of the churches in Iserlohn and surroundings) for the Friday edition. "Be careful, especially with the Catholic parishes. One mistake, and you lose subscribers."

Directing Christians to God at the right time was a hellish job! There were more than forty congregations in the town and its suburbs. The Protestant churches were less of a problem as long as I mentioned which of them celebrated Holy Communion the next Sunday. But, woe if I erred on the Catholic side. I was then, and still am, a world champion of typos. Sometimes, when Mass was at 10:30 a.m., I wrote 10:00 or 11:30 and didn't notice. On Monday, the office telephones rang all morning.

"You have put my salvation at risk," one old lady shouted.

"You did this deliberately, you despicable *Lutheran*," another caller averred; clearly, the ecumenical love I so enjoyed in France had not reached Westphalia yet.

Herr Künkler, himself a Catholic, made me visit every priest in town to apologize. With a few exceptions, I bowed to grim-faced clerics.

Worse was to come when I temporarily worked in Menden, where my boss was a sexy Lutheran woman from Bremen who sent me out to write a feature story about All Saints' Day. I made an appointment with the dean of the local parishes. When I entered his parsonage, he snarled,

"What do you want?"

"Please explain to me your customs on All Saints' Day. What do you do in your cemeteries?"

"What? Why don't you know this? Are you not a Christian?"

"I am, but I am a Lutheran, Reverend."

"What! Another Lutheran covering this Catholic town for a Christian Democrat newspaper? I'll complain to your publisher."

"Who is also a Protestant, Reverend!"

"Get out of this parsonage, you lout!"

He pushed me out of the front door.

Following this episode, I was swiftly transferred to Altena, a town in the Protestant part of the Sauerland, but I'll get to that later.

At this point, however, I am still in Iserlohn, where I learned the basics of my craft. Herr Künkler soon decided that the order of church services would be safer in the hands of his pedantic secretary. I had to be taught more important aspects of my craft, for example, how to write a news item.

The first piece of this basic genre was easy enough: In just two paragraphs, it told the story of a canary in the municipal lost-and-found office. The yellow bird must have left its cage, flown out of the window into a park, whence it couldn't find its way home.

"Bird-brained bird! Don't you dare to write that!" Künkler growled. "You are to write a simple news item about a canary in the lost-and-found bureau, not some goofy commentary on the intelligence of canaries."

"*Jawohl, Herr Künkler.*"

Then, my training took a more serious turn.

"Always start a story with the most essential information you are reporting, including its source," Künkler began. "Then follow up with the second, then the third, and then the fourth most important, and so forth. The least significant stuff belongs at the end so that the compositor can chop it away when your story in your manuscript is too long." Snappy punchlines, so common in modern journalism, were not possible in news pieces in the nineteen-fifties, four decades before the advent of computers, which make producing newspapers much more flexible.

When I learned my trade, newspapers were cobbled together much like in the nineteenth century. Manuscripts were sent to the typesetter, who keyed them into a linotype machine, which spawned lines of molten lead. These, in turn, went to the compositor, who placed them in a heavy steel frame called type chase and added headlines he had made by hand, following instructions from the newsroom.

"Different rules apply to feature stories. Now, you must use what I call the *sinus-cosinus* system. You begin with a high point (*sinus*), follow up with a bunch of factual information, taking your story to a low point (*cosinus*). Before readers get bored with too many facts, you weave in the next high point, and so on and so on. However, you must end your piece with a high point, a sinus, to make the reader smile or get him excited."

It wasn't easy, though, to find high and low points for the first feature story Herr Künkler sent me out to cover: It was a reportage about the opening of a new municipal swimming pool.

Herr Künkler also taught me what fonts to use. In Germany, they had names such as *Nonpareille*, *Petit*, *Borgis*, and then, depending on size, three, four, or five *Cicero*. He also showed me how to make a simple layout drawn with a crayon on an old newspaper page and how to write captions and headers. Ah, yes, and I had to develop films as well.

But how did I know what the most and the least important news item was? To learn this, Herr Künkler made me accompany him to cover a meeting of the city council, for example, and then sit next to him as he wrote his report.

All this helped prepare me for my next position in Altena, where I worked under—or, rather, in the stead of—Herr Exner, a charming, good-looking, but bone-idle man. Our newsroom was opposite the railway station. I arrived at eight in the morning, and he arrived at nine, equipped with a pack of liverwurst or cheese sandwiches, which he plonked on my desk as a bribe. Aloofly, he asked me how I intended to fill four to five local pages and then disappeared to the bedroom of his mistress, whom I had never met.

I wrote stories I had researched the evening before or that had come up during the day, such as a juicy murder or train derailment. I loved those because I could also file them to the Associated Press in Frankfurt for extra money. I also rewrote the boring manuscripts of stringers, usually schoolteachers. By 5:00 p.m. I packaged my manuscripts, pictures, and layouts and took them by train to Hagen, where the Altena edition was printed. Sometimes Herr Exner came by to check what I had done, but most often not. He took me for a beer and a

The author as trainee reporter in the Altena newsroom if the Westfalenpost. He did all the work whilst his had a merry time in his mistress' bedroom.

pea or lentil soup at the station restaurant, then boarded a train home to his wife.

I went back to the office, had a brief snooze, and subsequently went by taxi to one of the outlying villages to cover a meeting of a village council, a singing society, or some other club. My colleague Rolf, the intern of *Westfälische Rundschau*, a Social Democrat newspaper, went to events in a different municipality. His boss, too, didn't bother much with the office, not for reasons of lust but because, as an Altena city councilman, he was more interested in local politics. He never brought Rolf a sandwich or a beer. I couldn't stand him. Exner was a jolly human being, and Rolf's supervisor was a nasty ideologue.

Rolf and I exchanged carbon copies of our stories and then rewrote them so well that nobody except Herr Exner noticed. Exner laughed and invited Rolf to a beer.

My months in Altena were busy yet blissful. I loved working without serious supervision and earned extra money as an AP stringer because Altena and its surroundings always produced stories about fatal traffic accidents, derailed trains, plus the odd robbery or even one or two cases of manslaughter.

This joyful period of my training as a journalist ended after a few months when I was transferred to Olpe, a pretty town in the southernmost part of the Sauerland, where my main duty consisted of covering *Schützenfeste*, target shooting festivals going back to the Middle Ages. There was one in the surrounding towns and villages virtually every summer weekend, but the biggest such event took place in Olpe itself. It featured free beer from two different local breweries on Fridays and Saturdays, and that turned out to be a calamity for me.

On Saturday evening, I took my girlfriend, a lovely black-haired advertising saleswoman of the Social Democrat-leaning *Westfälische Rundschau*, to the *Schützenplatz* for booze and dance. We were accompanied by a singularly unattractive woman, "an acquaintance, not a friend" of my beloved beauty, as the latter whispered into my ear.

According to my girlfriend, I downed 58 beers that evening, then disappeared with her into the woods, or so I thought. Sunday morning, I woke up in my rented room in the station master's apartment in Olpe's railway depot, feeling the sting of pine needles all over the back of my body. Somebody was lying heavily on my right arm. I looked at her and, God help me, it was my girlfriend's ugly acquaintance.

Outside my door, my landlord and landlady were preparing to go to Sunday Mass. I held my hand over the woman's mouth, telling her to get out quickly once they were gone. Walking to my office, I ran into my girlfriend. She was grinning viciously.

"What happened?" I asked her.

"After 58 beers, you had the audacity to take me into the woods with you. Do you really think I would smooch with a drunken young man reeking of booze and cigarettes? This should teach you a lesson." It did, especially as the episode had an unpleasant aftermath.

The woman I bedded by mistake turned out to be the daughter of the district chairman of the Social Democrat Party. When I clumsily snubbed her attempt to continue our relationship, she told her father, who informed his Christian Democrat counterpart, who, in turn, reported it to his state chairman, deputy prime minister Artur Sträter, who then turned this matter over to his wife, Dorita, the CEO of *Westfalenpost*.

She was bemused by my mishap, but in the meantime, the news had spread all over Olpe. There was an uproar. The station master kicked me out of my room from one day to the next; scores of our readers threatened to cancel their subscriptions if I wasn't removed. So, I was. I ended up in Siegen, a town so ugly that Germans like to jest, "Question: what is worse than *verlieren* (to lose a conflict)? Answer: Siegen (to win)."

My stay in Siegen was short. I was assigned to the typesetting room to oversee the technical production of our local pages and those of neighboring *Westfalenpost* editions. Suddenly, I fell very ill. I could no longer breathe, felt too weak even to go to the office, and lost, most annoyingly, all my carnal desires.

In the hospital, I was diagnosed with a lead infection of the lungs. This came to the attention of the German Journalists' Association, which inquired whether, given that I was at that point still underage, I had been fed two liters of milk every day, as required by the collective bargaining agreement for trainees working in the lead-filled air of composing rooms. There was a lot of beer but no milk.

I was sent to a mountain resort to heal my lungs and, after six weeks, assigned to Neheim-Hüsten, which is also high in the Sauerland hills. My job was to be the sole editor of the Neheim-Nüsten edition for the rest of my internship. In fact, it was not really an internship anymore. In their negotiations with my union, the newspaper publisher agreed to elevate me to the rank of *Obervolontär* (senior trainee) with the duties and almost the same salary as a junior editor. The difference was only 50 DM.

In April, it was all over; I was a bona fide sub-editor. My employers wrote me a nice reference letter, regretting that I refused to stay with the company because, as a *Großstadtmensch*, a big-city person, I preferred to live and work in a metropolis. They even recommended me to *Frankfurter Neue Presse*, also a CDU-leaning paper.

But then my fate took a different turn.

Hitchhiking to Frankfurt on a Saturday in April 1958, I made a detour to Wiesbaden to attend my mother's performance in Händel's *Messiah*. Though a mezzo-soprano, she sang the alto part, including the oratorio's most beautiful aria.

The conductor raised his baton; I proudly turned around to watch Mutti step forward as a soloist in the gallery. She sang, "He was despised..." and then, oh horror, burst into tears, whimpering, "and rejected." She wept and sobbed. The conductor stopped the orchestra and asked a chorister to finish what Mutti had started.

The other people in my pew stared at me, knowing that this hysterical woman projecting the people's rejection of Jesus on her own persona was my mother.

"What happened?" a young woman next to me whispered.

"She is a very good singer but woefully self-centered," I stammered and slipped out.

I hitchhiked to Frankfurt and checked into a hotel room for only 5 DM a night. It was a sunny spring evening. I strolled up and down Kaiserstraße, the city's main street. On the corner of Moselstraße, I read the sign "The Associated Press GmbH." I walked up the stairs to the newsroom on the third floor and saw a youngish man in the center of a horseshoe-shaped desk.

"Who are you?" he asked me.

"Uwe Siemon-Netto."

"Ah, the intern filing hot stories from the Sauerland."

"Yes, except that my internship is now over."

"Good, what are you doing here?"

"Tomorrow morning, I'll have an interview with the editor of *Frankfurter Neue Presse*."

"Why go there if you could get a more exciting position right here with us at the AP? We are looking for a good young writer with a good news sense. You'll fit. Cancel your appointment and come by tomorrow morning at nine to meet Rudi Josten, our editor-in-chief. I'll prepare him."

I did. Josten hired me on the spot for a one-week trial period and subsequently gave me a contract with a monthly wage of 600 DM, 200 DM more than what I would have earned at a provincial newspaper. A few months later, my salary was raised to 1,000 DM.

Thus began the most exciting period of my professional life.

CHAPTER 11

Urchin's Last Years in Germany

I WAS HAPPY. NO sooner had I come of age than I had attained a job in international journalism. But a few weeks later, Andreas Szentmihályi dampened my exuberance. Andy, as his colleagues at the Associated Press called him, was a Hungarian nobleman running the domestic desk of the AP's German service in Frankfurt. He was permanently crabby, chiefly because of his stomach ulcers, a state he aggravated by spooning very spicy *gulyas* from a thermos flask every day.

Once, early in my AP days, he made me write a colorful reportage. I have forgotten what the topic was, but I still remember my sense of alarm as I watched him read the piece. Andy's face darkened, he rolled up my manuscript, slapped it around my ears, and snarled in his Hungarian burr, "*Ersparren Sie mir Ihrre unmaßgääbliche Meinung*" (spare me your irrelevant opinion). I never forgot this scene because I realized how right he was. Today, I wish there were an Andy in every newsroom!

Within a year, I sat in the slot of the horseshoe desk, assigning work to colleagues much older than I and editing their copy.

The author as slot editor in the AP newsroom in Frankfurt, 1958.

That year was the most contented in my professional life. I won praise from my superiors for the colorful style of my reportages. Now and then, the foreign editor sent me abroad to cover stories for which she deemed me most qualified, such as jazz. So, I went to Garches outside Paris for the funeral of the American soprano saxophonist and clarinetist Sidney Bechet (1897–1959), whom I had met during my stint in the French capital before my training at *Westfalenpost*.

Like Paris, Frankfurt had a lively jazz scene, including two musicians of world renown. They were brothers Emil and Albert Mangelsdorff. Emil (1925–2022) was a saxophonist, and Albert (1928–2005) was a trombonist who, as soon after the war as 1952, played with Louis Armstrong and Gerry Mulligan at the Newport Jazz Festival in Rhode Island.

In Frankfurt, both brothers starred at the Jazzkeller in Kleine Bockenheimer Straße, which still exists. I spent night after night there slurping on a small bottle of orange juice because that was all I could afford, not because I didn't earn enough but because I had to send half my salary to Mutti, who resolutely refused to look for a job.

"Why don't you?" I asked her. "You are still young. You have a brilliant high school diploma with an A in Latin, Greek, Hebrew, French, and English."

"Uwe, I am an artist; that's my calling," she replied. "The Nazis forbade me to attend university. Now, all I would find is a desk job. Ladies of our class don't do office work."

"So, what do women of 'our' class do?"

"Look after their husbands."

"You don't have a husband. You have divorced him, remember?"

"Well, then I could run your household."

And now I committed a grievous error. I said, "Alright, come to Frankfurt and cook for me." So, she came, cooked well, but turned my next two years into unmitigated hell. No sooner had she arrived in Frankfurt than she was at war with my landlady with whom I had been on excellent terms but who did not at all take kindly to Mutti's class conceit.

Moreover, it hadn't dawned on my mother that I was a grown-up now and the only money earner in our household. She called my superiors at the AP to inquire whether they were satisfied with my work. She tried to control my private life, screaming at me when I came home late from a night out with colleagues at Karrenberg, a hangout for journalists on Münchner Straße. One Friday, I returned early in the morning from a girlfriend Helga's flat and bought Mutti roses at the florist store in Frankfurt railway station, only to have them whipped around my face by my irate mother. Her anger persisted all weekend. She hissed and growled at me even in church, making me pray silently, "Lord, please put an end to this."

God took his time fulfilling my wish. As I waited, my father died in a Lindau hospital. His second wife, Käthe, called me in the office. When I came home, Mutti said,

"Vati is dead."

"Who told you?" I asked her.

The author (L) with his girlfriend Helga and three AP colleagues in the jounalists' hangout Karrenberg.

"He came to bid me farewell. He stood there in this corner of the kitchen, looking and smiling at me. He was no longer blind."

I went to his funeral. Before he was buried, the undertaker opened Vati's coffin for me. He lay there, suntanned as ever but with a broad smile on his face. I surmised that at the moment of death, he could see again, which made him look happy.

His death gave me a foretaste of freedom. Vati left me a few thousand marks, allowing me to buy a second-hand Citroën 2CV. I drove it to Saint-Tropez, where I regaled in the joy of life without mum, dancing with fabulous women in l'Esquinade, the most elegant nightclub on the Côte d'Azur, for as long as I saw fit—I, not my mother. I resolved to leave her at the earliest opportunity.

My moment of liberation occurred a year later, on the 13th of August 1961, arguably the saddest day in German postwar history. It was a Sunday, one of my days off that week. I was still fast asleep

The author with his first car, a Citroën 2CV, in St. Tropez on the Côte d'Azur.

The author with his fisherman friend Emile Pastorelli at the port of St. Tropez in France.

when Herbert Schmitt called early in the morning; he was the deputy editor-in-chief of the AP's German service.

"Get up. Come straight to the office to pick up your airline ticket," he said.

"Where am I going, Léopoldville?" I asked because I had volunteered to cover the civil war in the former Belgian Congo for the English-language service.

"No, you are going to Berlin. Ulbricht is closing the border and about to build a wall."

I wasn't surprised. For several months, I had written and edited articles about the intensifying Berlin crisis. Every day, 2,000 East Germans fled across the open border from East to West Berlin, especially professionals and highly skilled workers and craftsmen. In June, I was temporarily transferred to our Vienna bureau to move my American colleagues' copy about the summit conference between the young U.S. President John F. Kennedy and Soviet party leader and Prime Minister Nikita Khrushchev.

The AP White House correspondents covering this event told me that Khrushchev had developed an extremely low opinion of Kennedy, calling him a boy in shorts. The Soviet delegation in Vienna thought even less of Kennedy's snooty entourage of intellectuals, commonly taunted as "eggheads" in the U.S. capital, men like National Security Advisor McGeorge Bundy, Defense Secretary Robert MacNamara, and Secretary of State Dean Rusk. The Soviets correctly did not expect any reprisal from these people if Khrushchev allowed Ulbricht to seal off West Berlin, especially as Bundy was a renowned Germanophobe, and the president's relationship with West German chancellor Konrad Adenauer was tense.

Herbert Schmitt (L), deputy editor of the Associated Press German service in Frankfurt with two American colleagues studying the AP coverage of the construction of the Berlin Wall in a local newspaper. It was Schmitt who sent the author to Berlin.

So, on that 13th of August 1961, I boarded a piston-powered PanAm Douglas DC-6 to Tempelhof Airport in West Berlin, where I rented from Hertz a Ford Taurus and drove to Bernauer Straße, the center of the action before checking into my hotel. Bernauer Straße ran along the border between the Soviet and French sectors of Berlin.

For a stretch of 1.4 kilometers, the street was lined by apartment blocks with doors opening east whilst only windows faced the West Berlin side. Residents jumped out of these windows before men of the East German Workers Militia could brick them up. I watched the tenants leap into nets spun out for them by western firemen. It didn't take long for some refugees to miss their net and hurtle to their

On the 22nd of August 1961, Ida Siekmann (l), an East Berlin nurse, jumped from a fifth floor window to Bernauer Straße. (r) in the French sector, missed the net and died. She was the first victim of the Berlin Wall.

deaths. The first was Ida Siekmann, who died crashing on the sidewalk on the 22nd of August 1961; 139 more were to lose their lives at the Berlin Wall before it came down in November 1989.

I drove along Bernauer Straße to the Protestant Versöhnungskirche (Church of Reconciliation). The sanctuary stood in East Berlin, but the entrance was built in such a manner that it could be used from the west. The East German militiamen had already begun walling it in. Two comely college students from New York watched them, perplexed. I left the car and stood next to them.

"What are these men doing?" one asked me. "Don't they realize that the members of this parish will no longer be able to worship here?"

"That's just the point," I said. "Communists are atheists. They want to destroy the Church."

"We are Americans. Can we go to the other side?" the other student wanted to know.

The Protestant Versöhnungskirche (Church of Reconciliation) stood in East Berlin, but its entrance faced West. So, the Communists walled it in.

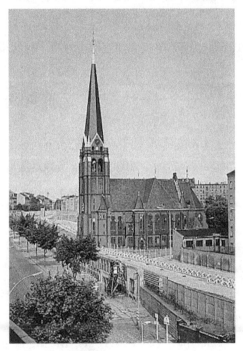

The Church of Reconciliation, including its bell tower.

A photo of Ida Siekmann

"I'm sure you can. But let's find out. Get into my car."

A West Berlin policeman stood nearby.

"These ladies are Americans. I have a West German ID card. Will the Communists admit us to their sector?" I asked him.

"Yes, they have just announced new rules," he replied. "Foreigners may cross over on Friedrichstraße, West Germans on Heinrich-Heine-Straße. West Berliners are, for the time being, forbidden to visit the Soviet sector."

I dropped the girls at what became known as Checkpoint Charlie and told them I would pick them up a few blocks from the border point for aliens. Then I drove on to Heinrich-Heine-Straße, which was not far.

"Let's go to a bar to meet East Berliners," suggested the two New Yorkers.

"Excellent idea. I must talk to them too for my story."

We found a pub filled with irate people, which provided me with plenty of copy about the public mood in their sector. Suddenly, they fell still. One of the most outspoken guests nodded to the door where two senior police officers had just entered and were now pushing themselves toward us.

"*Ausweise, bitte* (papers, please)," they ordered us.

"*Amerikanerinnen! Westdeutscher! Verlassen Sie dieses Lokal* (Americans! West German! Leave this bar)," the higher-ranking of the two, a major, demanded.

"Why?"

"It has come to our attention that your presence here is causing unrest."

"How?"

"You can clarify that at the station if you want," the major threatened. "But that will take several hours."

I decided to leave because I had to write my story, for which I now had ample material. The girls understood my decision. We agreed to meet later that night in Eden Saloon, a fashionable nightclub on Kurfürstendamm not far from the AP's Berlin office, where I filed my piece, one of my most successful articles with significant consequences. It appeared on August 14th in all West German and West Berlin newspapers.

It was also read in East German ministries, as I discovered late Monday night when the telephone rang in my West Berlin hotel room. The voice on the other end of the line was muffled because the female caller had clearly wrapped a silk stocking around her phone shell. But I knew who she was because she used the keyword Markt (market) we had agreed upon after meeting at the Leipzig International Spring Fair earlier that year.

Let's call her Gisela. She was about 35 when she caught my eye. Gisela worked for the East German foreign trade ministry. She stayed in a hotel; I stayed with Omi. We first saw each other in the Press Club on the top floor of the Messehaus am Markt. Before we met, though, I saw an exquisite woman sitting alone at a table. She smiled at me, and I smiled back. I asked, "May I join you?" She answered, "By all means." I kissed her right hand, sat down, and engaged her in a flirtatious conversation after noticing that she wore no wedding band.

"How dare you pick up my wife?" thundered a familiar male voice behind me, the voice of Karl-Eduard von Schnitzler, the vile host of the virulent anti-Western Schwarze Kanal (black channel) on East German television. West German viewers nicknamed him Sudel-Ede (besmirching Eddie).

"Go away, you are no longer my husband," said the lovely woman. He grabbed her by the right upper arm and yanked her out of the club room.

"You were trying to pick up the wrong woman, huh?" said a soft-spoken lady who turned out to be Gisela. "I sat over there at that table with West German businessmen but found your approach to one of our leading actresses far more interesting."

"Who is she?"

"Christine Laszar. She was indeed married to Sudel-Ede, but only briefly. Their marriage was short-lived."

Karl-Eduard von Schnitzler, East Germany's chief television propagandist. His program, called Der schwarze Kanal (the black channel) spewed hatred against the democratic West.

Karl-Eduard von Schnitzler years later.

Ballhaus Resi in West Berlin where comely lonely hearts could be picked up.

Ballhaus Resi Postcard.

"Sudel-Ede? You just used our nickname for Schnitzler!"

"Deliberately!"

Gisela and I became friends. It became obvious that she loathed the Communist regime even though she was one of its officials. When we parted, she told me, "Uwe, the situation in Berlin is getting queasy. Whatever happens, I'll try to contact you."

"How will you locate me?" I wanted to know.

"My office receives all Western newspapers. The origination of your byline and your dateline will tell me in which city I can find you. Once I know this, we have ways to find out where you are staying."

"Are you a spook?"

"Definitely not. However, I know how to use their services to establish contacts with Western businesspeople and reporters. So, if you receive a hushed telephone call and hear the word, Markt, you will realize that I am on the line, even if you don't recognize my voice."

Late in the evening of August 14th, the voice on my phone said "Markt" and instructed me to drive to a secluded spot on Müggelsee, the largest of Berlin's 3,000 lakes. It is vast, with an area of 7.4 square kilometers (2.9 square miles) and spectacular public beaches. But at the place she had chosen, we could be alone and unobserved, which was perfect for both of our desires, romantic and journalistic.

Gisela embraced me passionately. She had rented a rowboat, on which we traveled far from shore. I found her even more attractive than when we had met in Leipzig. But she was also full of useful information, not state secrets, but news about the lives and moods of her neighbors, all marvelous color for my reportages.

"Would you like to see Karl-Eduard von Schnitzler again, I mean live?" Gisela asked me.

"How?"

"He drives to West Berlin at least once a week."

"What for?"

"Pick up women in a ballroom."

"Which one?"

"Ballhaus Resi in der Hasenheide. Keep an eye open for him. He drives an ivory-colored Mercedes with East Berlin license plates and always crosses the border in the early evening at Checkpoint Charlie."

"The filthy sod! And he took umbrage when I flirted with his ex-wife in Leipzig, not knowing who she was."

"Expect your moment of payback."

"Can't wait."

The following week, I established an observation post for the Associated Press at Checkpoint Charlie. I found it while having a beer in a sleazy bar named Café Cölln on the right-hand side of Friedrichstraße, just before the demarcation line. Actually, it wasn't a café at all, but a front for a brothel. I had checked out the position of its easternmost window and found that it would allow us a perfect view of the traffic coming west from East Berlin and of the activities of the Communist border police.

I went upstairs and knocked on the door. A cuddly-looking woman in her late thirties opened, a 20-DM hooker, as we called her species. I held out a 100 DM note and asked her, "Why don't you do your business elsewhere? Surely, you won't find many clients at this place."

"Give me 150, and I'll move out," she replied. I agreed.

I placed a chair by the window and looked east through a pair of binoculars. I was jubilant. I saw an ivory-colored Mercedes with a license plate beginning with IA. There couldn't be too many of those in

East Berlin. I knew that my colleagues from other wire services were also watching from a building across the road. I signaled them to watch out for the Mercedes. The car rolled slowly to the U.S. passport control. I wished at that moment that Gisela was standing with me at the window. I would have hugged her thankfully: At the wheel of the car sat, as she had predicted, Karl-Eduard von Schnitzler—*Sudel-Ede*.

While soldiers at the American border control post checked his ID, I ran downstairs and started my car. The reporters of the other wire services did the same. Now, von Schnitzler drove into West Berlin. We followed him. He sped up his Mercedes. I had a hard time keeping up with him in my little Citroën 2CV, which another AP reporter had brought to Berlin from Frankfurt, fuming because it was so slow.

Sudel-Ede entered the Ballhaus Resi. We followed him. He occupied a table in the center of the ballroom; we positioned ourselves at tables close to his. All had large telephones with big numbers so that guests might call ladies with whom they wanted to dance. There were many more women than men in the room, some most desirable. Sudel-Ede tried to find a female companion but didn't succeed because we journalists took turns dialing his number and thus blocked it. We enjoyed our game hugely, but he didn't. After one hour, he gave up and walked out of Ballhaus Resi, puce in the face. We followed him, hooting. He returned east. In retrospect, I am a little ashamed of our childish behavior. But at the time, we felt gratified, having, in a small way, avenged the Western nations he besmirched Monday after Monday at 9:30 p.m. with his foul propaganda broadcast.

At about the same time, my career was beginning to take a turn. One day in late September, my old friend Eugen Vietinghoff asked me for a drink. I knew him from my apprenticeship at *Westfalenpost*, where he had been the sports editor. Now, he was managing editor of *BZ*, a local Berlin tabloid belonging to the Axel Springer group, Germany's largest publishing house.

"Uwe, I am just back from a conference of the top Springer editors in Hamburg where your name came up. Julius Hollos, the boss of the Springer Foreign News Service, especially took a keen interest. He asked me if you spoke English and another

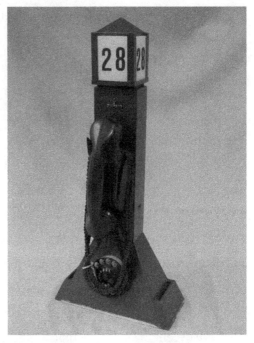

One of the table telephones in Ballhaus Resi. The author and other reporters blocked the number to deny East German "Sudel-Ede" Karl Eduard von Schnitzler access to West Berlin lonely hearts.

language well. I said, 'Yes, English and French, and Uwe told me once that he would like to become a foreign correspondent.' So, Hollos asked me for your telephone numbers. Expect a call from him."

A couple of days later, a man who sounded like Andreas Szentmihályi rang me at my hotel. Like Andy, Julius Hollos was Hungarian, except that he was also Jewish. Unlike Szentmihályi, he was the very opposite of crabby and was very funny. He invited me to lunch at the elegant executive dining room on the top floor of the Axel Springer skyscraper overlooking the Berlin Wall.

Julius was a big man. He told me how much he loved the position he had held before World War II. He was the cultural editor of *Prager Tagblatt*, a top-quality German-language newspaper in the Czechoslovak capital. Just as the Germans were about to invade, he fled to London. After the war, he joined the Axel Springer Corporation and founded its foreign news service.

"Uwe, I hear you would like to be a foreign correspondent," he said straight out. "I can offer you London, Paris, or New York." I don't know why, but I answered, "London, please, Herr Hollos."

"When can you start? We first would like you to spend a month at our head office in Hamburg. You may start tomorrow."

"Herr Hollos, the AP has been a very fair employer, so I must also treat them fairly and give them three months' notice."

"Very decent of you. I like that. December 1st, then." He shook my hand.

Now, I had to tell my mother that I was going to London without her. Yes! Without her!

"How am I going to live?" she asked on the telephone.

"You are still young. Find a job. I have to focus on my career."

Before leaving Berlin, I had a frightening experience on October 25th, my 25th birthday. The night before, Gisela rang, saying, "*Fahre schnell zum Kronprinzen-Palais* (rush to the former Prussian crown prince's palace)." I drove across the border at seven o'clock and saw Soviet soldiers laying telephone cables along the sidewalks and unmarked Red Army T-54 tanks rolling into the building's courtyard. I quickly returned to my office on Fasanenstraße and asked U.S. military government officials for comment. A member of the CIA station just said, "My God, this will lead to a dangerous confrontation; until now, no Soviet armor had entered Berlin."

I filed my story in German and English. In the evening, we received what was called the "play message" from New York. It told us how our stories had run in the American newspapers, radio, and television stations. My piece, a news item without a byline, was used by all AP subscribers in the U.S., to which the head office added the three words "flowers to Uwe."

"Flowers" was meant to be a compliment in wire service lingo, whereas "rockets" indicated a criticism. Play messages were transmitted between the head office and overseas bureaus via an internal

Soviet and American tanks confronting each other at Checkpoint Charlie in October 1961. The author's East Berlin friend Gisela tipped him off that this was about to occur.

wire, which the AP management assumed no outsider could read. This was naïve, as I discovered two days later.

On the morning of October 27th, the predicted standoff between Soviet T-54 and U.S. M-48 tanks happened at Checkpoint Charlie. In the late afternoon, I tried to cross to the East at Heinrich-Heinrich-Straße for a rendezvous with Gisela. I was immediately arrested and taken to a backroom by two Stasi officers. They drove me away to a station, stripped me of my belt and my watch, and locked me into a windowless and unlit cell.

I remembered what I had been told a year earlier in an intelligence course about exactly such a situation. "When they lock you up and take your watch, try to keep track of the time," the instructor said. "The German way of counting will be most helpful. Say in your head *einundzwanzig, zweiundzwanzig* (twenty-one, twenty-two), and so on, and each number will correspond exactly to one second. Use your fingers when you count time in your cell. Try to do so by keeping your hands on your laps if your inquisitors allow you to." In my case, they did.

"You were the reporter who first filed the story about the arrival of the Soviet tanks," the senior interrogator, a lieutenant colonel, said.

"What gives you this idea?" I retorted.

"We know that you crossed over early Wednesday morning."

"I do this very often."

"Yes, but you were seen driving along Unter den Linden."

"Again, as I do frequently. Unter den Linden is a beautiful boulevard."

The conversation went on and on until I noticed that the Stasi officers were getting frustrated. They took me back into my cell, where I continued counting time diligently.

Early Sunday morning, one of the two, a lieutenant colonel, unwisely lost his temper.

"We have evidence that this story was yours," he said. "Now, tell us what your source was, and we will let you go."

"What evidence?"

He pulled a neatly folded paper out of his tunic and pushed it under my face; it was the "play message" from the AP head office in New York. With his fat middle finger, the officer pointed at the words "flowers to Uwe" and growled, "Doesn't this mean that your bosses praised you for a story?"

"They praised somebody called Uwe for something, period. And now you have revealed to me that you are reading our internal wire correspondence."

The two Stasi men stared at me aghast. I went on:

"It's Sunday morning. I am on Sunday duty. At eight o'clock I must be in my office. If I am not, my colleagues will know that something has happened to me, for they knew that I had driven East on Friday. May I remind you that all of Berlin is still subject to the Four-Power Statute and that in this city, the AP falls under the supervision of the U.S. military government. My detention here will cause an international crisis because, in a sense, I am an employee of the Americans."

At 4:00 a.m., the Stasi officers discharged me, handed me the key to my car, and accompanied me to Checkpoint Charlie, where they advised the East German border guards to let me pass, especially because Heinrich-Heine-Straße was still closed so early in the morning.

Two weeks later, Mutti called me to tell me about a secret message from Omi in Leipzig. It said that I must never again try to enter

The border crossing at Heinrich-Heine-Straße reserved for West Germans visiting East Berlin where the author was arrested by the Stasi.

East Germany, with the exception of East Berlin. If I did, I would be arrested and charged with treason.

The two women had developed a smart system to communicate. Omi baked a cake for Mutti, but first placed her message in a small glass tube and slipped it into the dough. Mutti, on the other hand, hid her information in a *Frikadelle*, the German equivalent of a hamburger, because good meat was rare in East Germany at the time.

Much later, I met Omi on holiday in West Germany (the Communist regime allowed its residents to visit the West after their 65th birthday).

"Who had tipped you off?" I asked her.

"A people's prosecutor was living in our house. For some reason, she liked me and didn't want me to lose my grandson for what might have been decades."

When I discussed with Mutti my impending transfer to London without her, she asked dolefully, "How am I going to live?"

"Well, work, Mutti. There are plenty of jobs for educated women like you."

As it turned out, Mutti had a different idea. She studied the advertising pages of newspapers and discovered a German emigrant by the name of Murschall. He lived in New Hampshire and manufactured aluminum window frames. Herr Murschall was a widower and now tried to find a new wife via newspaper advertisements.

I met him in my Frankfurt apartment when I paid Mutti a farewell visit at Christmas 1961 before driving to London. He seemed a pleasant, good-looking man. Mutti and Murschall had married in my absence. She already had her U.S. immigrant visa, and Murschall had bought her a ticket for an elegant German ocean liner that would bring Frau Murschall to the United States.

At Christmas, while Murschall rose to relieve himself and Mutti and I enjoyed the candle lights reflecting on the gold tinsel of the tree, she whispered, "He was only a sergeant major in the war, you know?"

After this remark I was even happier to drive my funny French car to the ferry boat at Ostend in Belgium! My joy was short-lived, though. A few days after I arrived in London, I received a letter from Mutti accusing me of pushing her, a staff officer's daughter, into the arms of a mere former sergeant major. She had filed for divorce. She insisted that I paid for it. I sent her 800 DM and informed her that, from now on, my salary was mine and mine alone. With that, I entered an exciting new life that evolved into a nearly 60-year marriage.

Printed in the USA
CPSIA information can be obtained
at www.ICGtesting.com
JSHW020421071024
70968JS00003BA/7/J